THE EARTH FOR SAM

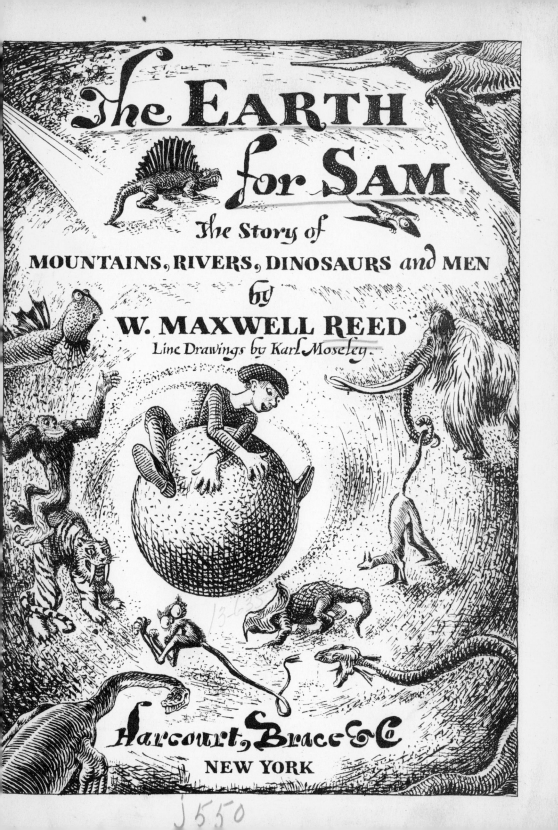

The EARTH for SAM

The Story of
MOUNTAINS, RIVERS, DINOSAURS and MEN
by
W. MAXWELL REED
Line Drawings by Karl Moseley

Harcourt, Brace & Co
NEW YORK

PRINTED IN THE UNITED STATES OF AMERICA
BY THE KNUDSEN PROCESS

DEDICATED
TO MY MOTHER
EMILY PUTNAM REED

PREFACE

My small nephew, Samuel McCobb Reed, used to ask me to tell him about the formation of rivers, mountains, and clouds and about the earth and stars. Since obviously such questions cannot be answered briefly and since my time was limited on week-end visits, I told Sam I would write him letters. Some of the chapters in this book are these letters almost unmodified. My friends suggested that I complete the series of letters and publish them in book form.

If this book is enjoyed by its readers and if the information it gives is accurate and in logical sequence, it is largely due to the author's good fortune in having two very good editors. Miss Jannette M. Lucas, Librarian of the Osborn Library of Palaeontology at the American Museum of Natural History, edited the manuscript both for scientific accuracy and also for proper sequence in which the many events should be recorded. Like that titanic force that moved the Matterhorn sixty miles into strange lands, Miss Lucas took chapters and moved them bodily to other locations. Then they were eroded and smoothed by my wife's editing until now only a scholar, adept in the Bacon-Shakespeare controversy, could tell whence those chapters came.

PREFACE

To my friend, Karl Moseley, I am deeply indebted for those unique "tailpieces" and for the cover design. Also this artist as well as many other friends helped to wear away those original folds that made the now weathered chapters from which I hope the grammatical canyons and crags have been eliminated.

The task has been made easier by the excellent work of Mr. George F. Brelsford who did all the typing and made many corrections. Also I wish to thank those cordial librarians of the American Museum of Natural History for their patience in providing me with innumerable books from that very excellent library and giving my notes temporary parking space upon the shelves.

If the author had been the political boss of the Palaeolithic Age, he would have required "hall marks" on all artifacts and to assist archaeologists further he would have ordained that the design of the mark be changed every ten thousand years. An excellent alternative, however, is the friendship of Mr. N. C. Nelson, Associate Curator of Archaeology of the American Museum of Natural History, who arranged a choice collection of stone tools in chronological sequence for the author's information.

Of course Sam is growing older all the time, but Miss Amy Loveman, Associate Editor of the *Saturday Review of Literature*, pointed out that I had assumed an unusually rapid rate of maturing for a normal white primate; for if the first chapter assumed Sam's age at perhaps eight

PREFACE

years, the last chapter certainly assumed a grammar
school stage of development. To some extent Mrs. Reed
has reduced Sam's rate of aging by making the first chapters a little more mature, but even now Sam and his associate readers must grow old together as they climb
through the chapters of rising and falling mountains with
the dragons of the air and the monsters of the sea.

W. MAXWELL REED.

July 3, 1928.
Sound Beach, Connecticut.

CONTENTS

THE EARTH FOR SAM

I. WHEN THE EARTH WAS HOT

A LONG, very long time ago, the earth was hot; so hot that the water boiled and the sky was full of steam. There were no plants, no animals, and no fishes. Nothing could live on account of the heat.

In some places the rocks had melted and streams of thick white-hot lava flowed over the land and into the water. Of course, there was no one there to see the great clouds of steam that rose up to the sky when all this melted rock flowed into the sea.

The uprushing steam caused thunder storms, so that the sky was full of lightning, and if any one had been there they would have heard loud roars of thunder nearly all the time.

The clouds were so thick that the sunlight never reached the earth. If you had been there, you would have

Suppose you had been there!

[3]

found that most of the light came from flashes of lightning and from the white-hot molten rock that flowed over the land and into the boiling sea; and the roar of the thunder would have been deafening.

Besides the thunder that was roaring all the time something else happened which would have been very dangerous if you had been there. Many big shooting stars rushed through the steaming air and struck the earth. They made even a louder noise rushing along than all the boiling oceans, and could be heard even above the thunder.

These shooting stars, many of which were as large as one of the big cities you see today, were white-hot. Because they were so hot they were blindingly bright, and for a few seconds, just before they struck the earth or rushed into the ocean, they were reflected in the great clouds of steam until it looked as if the sun were shining among the clouds.

You know that sometimes when two rocks hit each other very hard, sparks are made. When these great stars hit the earth not only were there thousands of sparks, but the very ground was melted, and the melted rock, white-hot like the stars themselves, splashed over everything. So hard did they strike the earth that even hills were thrown about as if they, as well as the rocks, were only pieces of mud, and for hundreds of miles the ground would shake and tremble.

When these shooting stars fell into the sea they made great waves, higher than our big buildings, and these waves would dash over the shores, and melted rocks and water swirled as in a great storm. No animals or plants could have lived in the smother of steam hanging like a cloud over everything. Sometimes the steam when it got high in the sky would cool and turn into rain, but when the drops of water fell upon the hot rocks they were again turned into steam.

The earth at first was small, but millions of these shooting stars, both great and small, which crashed down from the sky, kept making the earth a little larger each year. Finally, after long ages, there were hardly any big shooting stars left, and the earth stopped growing. Then it had a chance to cool and the water in the ocean stopped boiling. The great clouds of steam no longer rose high into the air, and little patches of blue sky appeared.

Very, very slowly the rocks became cool and the clouds scattered so that the bright sunlight came down upon both the land and the water. The rain from the clouds was no longer turned into steam by the hot rocks. It reached the earth and flowed off the land in streams and rivers as it does today.

How do we know the earth was formed in this way? Not a living thing, not even a piece of seaweed was anywhere on the earth at that time (Figure 1). However, for various reasons many men who have devoted their lives to the study of the earth, think that it was formed in this way. Of course they may be wrong, for, after all, mankind has only just begun to discover the answer to these

Courtesy of the Field Museum of Natural History

BEFORE LIFE CAME TO THE EARTH

Figure 1. No living thing in the sea or on the rocks. Neither moss nor seaweed existed then. After a painting by C. R. Knight in the Field Museum of Natural History, Chicago, Illinois.

great questions. Some English scientists think the earth was formed in a somewhat different manner, and a number of American geologists and astronomers agree with them.

The other theory is that the earth was once a huge ball of melted liquid rock and that it was then about the same size as it is now. At that time there were no big shooting stars, for all the rock and iron had been used up in making that enormous ball of melted rock which we call the earth.

Then slowly, very slowly, the earth began to cool. For a long time the crust of the earth was so hot that no water could stay on the surface—it was boiled and turned to steam and made huge clouds in the sky. Finally as the land cooled the water accumulated in the low places and the ponds grew into lakes and the lakes into oceans. During all this time the lightning must have been blinding and the thunder deafening, but there was no living thing in all the earth to see or hear.

Some day astronomers will tell you that once upon a time the sun had a collision with another star or at least came very near hitting another star which was wandering through space. Due to this meeting, huge masses of melted rock and fiery gases were broken away from our sun.

From this time there comes the difference of opinion which we have just described. Some think that the parts which were broken away from the sun at once formed

THE FIRST HOME OF THE LITTLE GERMS

Figure 2. They didn't realize that some day their descendants would live in skyscrapers. From a painting by
C. R. Knight.

millions of those little bodies that we call shooting stars. From time to time these little bodies met in collision and kept falling together until finally the great ball we call the earth was formed.

On the other hand, some astronomers claim that the pieces of the sun, white-hot and fiery, almost at once formed a huge ball of melted rock—the earth.

For years to come it may not be decided which of these two descriptions of the origin of the earth is correct. You may be sure, however, that during those years many will be working hard to find out the truth. The hunting for more knowledge about the history of the earth is even more interesting than reading about it after it has been discovered. As you read these chapters you will find there are many important things we do not know. Perhaps some day you may assist the hunters for knowledge and add your bit to the known history of the earth.

Now a curious thing happened. Little germs appeared in the water, which was still warm even if it were not boiling. These germs were so small that if you had been there with a magnifying glass you could not have seen them. They were floating around in the fresh water of the ocean, for the sea was not salt in those days. Perhaps the little germs were first formed in the soft warm mud near the edge of some shallow sea (Figure 2).

These little germs were the only living creatures on the earth. The land was only rock and mud and there was not a blade of grass, nor a flower, nor a tree—all over the earth only jagged rocks. Here and there great streams of melted rock were still coming from below the ground. Now and then the land would be shaken by an explosion as some volcano would blow fire high into the air and send streams of white-hot melted lava down its sides.

At first the ocean must have been a very dangerous place for these little germs. They couldn't swim and they couldn't see—just little specks floating in the warm water, but so small you couldn't have seen them with a magnifying glass, or even with the most wonderful microscope that has ever been made.

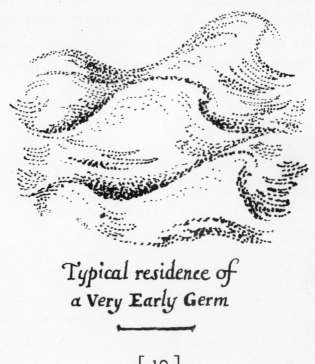

Typical residence of
a Very Early Germ

WHEN THE EARTH WAS HOT

Sometimes hundreds of them were carried by the swift currents in the ocean to some place where the hot lava was still coming up from the ground and making the water boil. The tiny germs couldn't endure boiling water any better than we can, so hundreds of them were killed by being scalded. Then, once in a while, large waves would carry them deep into the ocean where it was dark, because the sunlight couldn't get through so much water. The darkness and the great weight of the water pressing against them killed the germs almost as quickly as the boiling water. Yet as fast as some were scalded and some were killed by darkness, others appeared to take their places, so that there were always thousands of these little creatures floating near the surface of the ocean in the warm and sunny water in those times of long ago.

II. THE AIR WE BREATHE

IF YOU had come to the earth in those days and tried to walk on the rocks you would have suffocated. There was plenty of air, but even a dog would have panted for breath and then died; for the air was not good to breathe.

Before we go on and learn about the adventures of germs, let's try to find out about this air which we breathe and which was just as necessary to most of those early germs as it is to us.

In the first place, you look right through it and walk right through it; so that you have sometimes probably thought it was nothing. When you get into a strong wind you realize the air has such force that it will almost blow you over. An electric bulb has no air in it. If you weigh one of these bulbs on some very good scales, so that the bulb on one side of the scale will just balance the weight on the other side, and then if you make a very tiny hole in the bulb so as to let in the air, you will find that the bulb weighs more. The side of the scale holding the bulb will go down, which shows that when you let in the air you increased the weight of the bulb. Therefore, the air has weight—very little to be sure, but then there is a great deal of air, so that the total weight of all the air is very large. It is because air has weight that it is able sometimes to blow the branches off the trees and to make it hard for you to run against the wind.

The hardest thing of all is to understand just what air is. The air is made of millions of very little particles—so small that you cannot see them even with a microscope. They are smaller even than germs. When you go out in a strong wind, millions of these little atoms blow against you and make it hard for you to walk. When millions of them blow against a branch of a tree with great force, they make the branch bend and swing from side to side until it begins to crack and then, perhaps, it will break and fall to the ground.

All these little atoms are not alike. There are several kinds of atoms that are quite different from each other. You know there are many different kinds of dogs. Some dogs run very fast and won't come near you, while other dogs are very friendly and follow you everywhere. Most of the air we breathe is made of two kinds of atoms. One kind is called oxygen and the other kind is called nitrogen. If you can't remember the word oxygen, perhaps you can remember its nickname O. This isn't the figure zero; it is the letter O. In the same way, the nickname for nitrogen is N. Those who don't know atoms very well call them oxygen and nitrogen but those who are well acquainted with atoms call them O and N. We call oxygen (O) a gas, nitrogen (N) a gas, and we say that the air is mostly made of two gases, oxygen (O) and nitrogen (N).

These gases are just as different as the two kinds of dogs we just described. O is a very friendly gas and likes to join other atoms and go with them, while N likes to be by itself and is very slow to join with other atoms. The sociable gas O is very valuable to us, for it is the gas that keeps us alive when we breathe. We cannot live unless we are breathing O all the time. Animals and plants must have O all the time or else they die. When the doors and windows are closed, we say that the room is "stuffy." That is because we have used up part of the atoms of O. So we open a window and let in some fresh air which contains a new supply of millions of little atoms of O.

There is another very funny set of atoms called carbon, whose nickname is C, and this is the last set of atoms that you will have to remember for a long time. These atoms behave in a very strange way. A diamond is pure carbon (C) ; also coal is C. Some day you will learn why these two things both made of C look so different. When one atom of C is all alone in the air, two little atoms of the friendly oxygen immediately join it to keep it company. Sometimes millions and millions of these little groups of three atoms are formed and float in the air. They are so small that they are perfectly invisible, just like our friends O and N. If you want to talk about these groups of C and O you can call them CO_2—pronounced C-O-two. This name shows just what the gas is made of, for it says there are one atom of carbon and two atoms of oxygen. You write the 2 a little below the line and after the O so as to show that two of the friendly atoms of O came together to keep the one atom of C from feeling lonely.

CO_2 and perhaps N came from volcanoes and still come from those that are overflowing with streams of lava from time to time, for lava is full of gas. It may seem strange for gases to come from hot melted rock, but if you take a glass of water and let it stand for some time you will find that little bubbles of air have collected upon the sides of the glass. That means that the air was in the water and that when the water had been quiet for a time the air came out and clung to the sides of the glass; that is, the gases you call N and O came from the water and collected in little bubbles that you can see. In this same way when hot melted rock comes out of the volcanoes, gases of N and CO_2 bubble out and help to increase the air in the world. You know, however, that this air isn't good to breathe; for you must have O in the air in order to live, and so must most of the plants and animals.

Perhaps a little of this O has always been in the air since the hot rocks cooled and let sunlight reach the surface of the earth. However, most of our oxygen comes from that gas CO_2. In the next chapter we will learn how the plants break up the CO_2 and let the atoms of O go free.

From year to year you may read in books and magazines more about the origin of the air. If those Englishmen are correct in thinking that the earth very early in its life was a great ball of melted rock, then it is probable that it started even at that early date with a lot of atoms of N in the sky and a few atoms of O. Then more atoms came from the boiling lava in the volcanoes and formed our air.

N's such an unsociable chap.

III. SEAWEED AND JELLYFISH

LET US now return to those little germs that we left drifting around in the stormy seas of the newly made earth. Slowly, very slowly, they began to grow larger. The larger they grew the better chance they had to live, for it was hard to live in those troublous times. After a while they could just barely have been seen by the aid of a good microscope. That shows how very, very tiny they were in the beginning. Those that became large enough to be seen we call bacteria.

Some bacteria learned how to swim, and so they could hunt for food and keep away from dangerous places. Others made shells in which they could hide from their enemies. We call them shellfish. Still others clung to the rocks and became seaweed and beautifully colored coral. But it took hundreds of millions of years for the bacteria to make these changes in their appearance and ways of living, and in all this time some of them never changed at all, and their descendants stayed bacteria down to the present day. These changes were some of the queer things about life on this earth. We can tell you why some of these things happened, but there are some we know very little about. Perhaps some day you will hunt in the rocks for very old animals, and then maybe you can discover why some have changed their shape when others have not.

About 1,000 million years ago a group of bacteria were washed upon the shore and got covered with mud. Then the mud turned into rock, and a few years ago some of

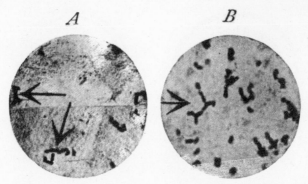

Courtesy of Charles Scribner's Sons

BACTERIA

Figure 3. *A*. Fossil bacteria which lived in Montana many millions of years ago. *B*. Living bacteria. From *Origin and Evolution of Life* by H. F. Osborn.

this rock was discovered in Montana by Charles D. Walcott of the U. S. Geological Survey. When the rock was split open these little bacteria were found; they were all turned to rock. Figure 3-A is a picture of these very old bacteria. Also Figure 3-B shows some bacteria that are living today. You can see how little the bacteria of today differ from those of long ago, when life was just starting on this earth.

CO-OPERATION AMONG THE CELLS

During all this time there was a fierce struggle among bacteria to keep alive, for there were hot currents in the ocean and cold currents, and waves and ice and steam. Some of the bacteria grew into little round cells like those in Figure 4. At first they were very simple like the cell marked A. Then they grew with a little dark head like

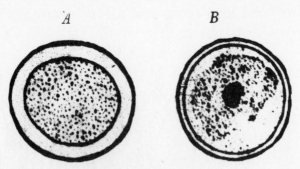

A VERY REMOTE ANCESTOR

Figure 4. This is a picture of the way a very simple cell looks through a magnifying glass. One of our ancestors looked like this many hundreds of millions of years ago. He must have been very proud of himself, for he was so much larger than those very tiny germs of life that lived in the warm water when the big shooting stars stopped falling. After a drawing in *Evolution of the Plant Kingdom* by M. C. Coulter (*Nature of the World and of Man*).

the picture marked B. They were and are nearly transparent, as we know because many of their descendants are living today just as their ancient ancestors did. They are bluish green and look like very tiny particles of jelly.

Perhaps one of the most interesting things that ever happened on this earth was when the little cells got together in groups and divided the work, so that each cell

[19]

had its own job to attend to and didn't have to do a little of everything. When you play games you usually divide the work—some of you guard the goal, while others run with the ball, some pitch the ball, and others spend most of their time catching it. When you divide work like that you can play many kinds of games. It was the same way with those little groups of cells. As soon as they divided up the work they found there were many ways of getting food and protecting themselves from danger.

Some of the groups of cells found that they could get their food better by floating about in the water. They didn't think very much about it. They merely kept on floating because the germs from which they had descended had always floated. When they became cells and then when they formed groups of cells they still kept on floating. Certain cells, however, could do some things better than the others could. Those on the outside could form a surface that protected the cells on the inside. Perhaps those on the inside were busy all the time getting food from the water.

Of course these groups of cells didn't get together and have a meeting and elect some one to act as president. They didn't appoint certain cells to do the eating and others to form a skin or shell and do the protecting, and still others to form fins and tails and do the swimming. That is the way we would do it today, but we are talking of a time 1,000 million years ago, and these cells had never done any thinking—worse even than that, they were deaf, dumb, and blind. Yet these groups of cells developed after millions of years into wonderful animals which could see and hear and talk. They did it very simply by just experimenting. These experiments were serious, for if they didn't succeed the cells usually died, and sometimes the whole group of cells died. They didn't know that they were experimenting, for they had no head and no brain. The experimenting was done in the following way:

All groups of cells were not exactly alike. Some were a little tougher than others, and some could absorb more atoms of gas from the water than others. If the tough cells happened to be on the outside layer of the group and the good eaters on the inside, then that particular group lived a little more comfortably than its neighbors. It wasn't so apt to get hurt, and it got food when perhaps its neighbors went hungry. When the waves and ocean currents carried groups of cells against the rocks, those groups that had a tough outer layer stood a better chance of surviving. Since children are usually like their fathers and mothers, the descendants of the little groups of cells with tough outer layers were usually made in the same way. So there grew up a number of groups of cells in which the outer layer was tough. Those groups of cells where by chance the outer layer happened to be very soft were often damaged and destroyed. Their descendants inherited the soft outside layer so that many of them were also killed. And so after a while—thousands of years—

all the groups of this particular kind would have a tough outer layer, and there would be none with a soft outside layer. Some of these groups of cells grew together to form that curious stuff we now call seaweed.

The seaweed grew in the shallow water of the ocean and at the mouths of rivers. It was seaweed that first gave us most of the very necessary gas, oxygen, which we have called O. For millions of years the green leaves and grass on the land and the seaweed in the ocean have given us quantities of atoms of O, so that now one-fifth of the air consists of O. How they do it is more or less of a mystery, but the general method is as follows:

When some groups of cells found they could live by attaching themselves to the rocks they developed a remarkable appetite. Some of the cells that did the eating caught the CO_2 which was dissolved in the water, swallowed the C, and spit out the O. Cells that can behave in this queer way are so complicated that we don't know just how they are made. They are bright green and are called chlorophyll. The C which the chlorophyll eats makes the stems tough and the trunks and branches of trees hard. It is the chlorophyll which gives the green color to most leaves and to the grass, as well as to nearly all seaweeds.

After millions of years the shallow water of the seas and rivers became very crowded. It was natural, therefore, that some seaweeds should try to get out of the water and live in the air. They didn't say to their friends,

A BOLD SEAWEED EXPLORES THE AIR

"Let's go and explore the air," just as some of us might say, "Let's go and try to explore Mt. Everest." No one said anything. It took the seaweeds a long time to accomplish it, for they had to have water as well as light in order that their chlorophyll could eat the CO_2. Of course they got plenty of light as soon as they poked their leaves out of the water, and also they found a quantity of CO_2 in the air; but they had to be very careful not to dry up when they were lying in the sun. Perhaps they first got accustomed to the air by lying on the mud flats for a few hours each day when the tide had gone out. Some day you will study astronomy and learn why the tides were probably greater in those days than now. The mud flats at low water were larger than now, so that there was plenty of room for some of the seaweed to get accustomed to the air as it lay in the wet pools on the sand for several hours each day.

As the leaves of the seaweed lay flat in the sun they wouldn't dry up so quickly if the upper layer of cells were tough and formed a kind of skin. Since this would be an advantage for seaweeds growing on mud flats, those plants that happened to have these tough cells on the upper surface would be more apt to live and their children would live after them.

After thousands of years a seaweed was developed that had some very clever devices. In order to keep moist, the cells on the under side of the leaf became elongated and poked themselves into the ground so that they could

[23]

absorb moisture and give it to the rest of the leaf. This was the very beginning of roots for plants and trees. The upper cells formed a tough layer to keep the moisture that was inside from getting out. The green chlorophyll was just under this tough layer or skin. You remember, how-

The Landing of the Seaweed
"on a stern and rockbound coast"

ever, that chlorophyll must have light in order to absorb CO_2, keep the atoms of C prisoners, and let the atoms of O go free. Consequently those leaves that had an outer layer of cells which was so thick that the light couldn't go through soon died. Only those seaweeds lived which happened to have an upper layer of cells that would let the light through. After a while all the leaves had a thin layer of cells on the outside that would let in light but would not let the leaf dry up.

So far the seaweed had done fairly well. It had got out of its crowded ocean for at least a few hours each day. It had developed an outer layer of cells that let the light through to the chlorophyll and yet kept the moisture inside the leaf. It had developed the cells on the bottom so that they grew long and went into the mud to get moisture for the leaf. There is one thing, however, that we haven't considered, and that is, how did the CO_2 get to the green chlorophyll? Although the outer layer was thin and would let in the light, it wouldn't let any gas like CO_2 get to the green chlorophyll. When the seaweed was in the ocean it didn't have this trouble, for some of the CO_2 was dissolved in the ocean, and the seaweed under the water didn't have such a tough outer layer of cells. The seaweed was soaked with water, and the chlorophyll absorbed the CO_2 from the water. On the land, however, the chlorophyll must get the CO_2 from the air or else the plant would die. Probably many plants did die for this very reason.

If some plants by chance had little openings in the tough outer layer of cells, the CO_2 would get through and be absorbed by the green chlorophyll. Plants, like groups of cells and like fishes, are not all just alike. Each individual plant is a little different from its brothers and sisters, just as we are a little different from our brothers and sisters. Perhaps, then, some members of the seaweed families happened to have little holes in this outer layer of tough cells, so that the CO_2 could get through to the chlorophyll. These plants would have a great advantage over their brothers and sisters and cousins. They could stay longer in the air without suffocating for lack of CO_2. After thousands of years the only plants that were high out of the water on the banks of the rivers down near the seashore were the seaweeds that could let CO_2 get through the little holes in the tough outer layer of cells.

If you had been there you would have been discouraged as you watched the plants for perhaps a million years trying to live in the air and never succeeding, for when there was a long hot and dry season, the little holes or pores in the leaves let the moisture escape and the plant would dry up and die.

Finally some plants grew which happened to differ in a very fortunate way from their neighbors. In these plants the outer layer of cells behaved very differently on a dry sunny day from the way it did on a wet rainy day. This is rather natural, for even now we don't behave on a hot sunny day just as we do on a cold rainy day. On a hot dry day the outer cells of these peculiar plants crowded together and accidentally closed up those little pores through which the CO_2 got to the chlorophyll. That was rather bad for the plant in one way, for it temporarily prevented the CO_2 from getting inside. This stopping of the pores, however, was also good for the plant, for it kept the moisture from escaping and kept the plant from becoming too dry. As soon, however, as the air became moist—at night or on a rainy day, that is—the cells would separate a little. The little pores then became open once more so that the CO_2 could go through and be absorbed by green chlorophyll. Such plants, in which the outer layer of cells would expand in moist weather and contract in dry, would be able to live much longer away from the water. Since the plants that didn't have this characteristic died, it is plain that all seaweeds that got out of the water and tried to live on the land had these expanding and contracting pores.

In Figure 5 you will find a picture of a plant that is, perhaps, like one of these primitive plants that emerged from the sea about 500 million years ago. Like so many other things we have read about, there are still plants today that are apparently almost like their primitive ancestors. The picture shows the way the plant would look if you took a knife and cut through the leaf and then looked at the edge through a microscope. On top you can see that the skin consists of a row of tough single cells. Then you can see a little opening that closes up during a hot dry day and opens during the moist night or during a rainy day. It must have been a rainy day when this picture was taken, for the little pore is open. Underneath the skin you can see the dark green cells that contain the chlorophyll. The CO_2 comes in through this pore and is eaten by the chlorophyll cells. At the bottom of the picture are the cells that have grown long so that they can get water from the moist earth and pass it along to the other cells and the chlorophyll. Of course, you will remember, the cells are so small they cannot be seen with

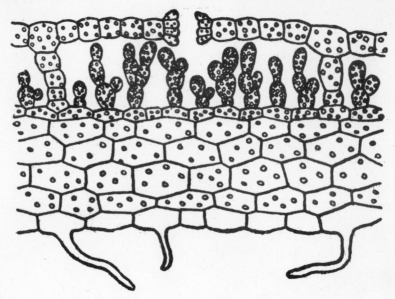

Courtesy of the University of Chicago Press

THE FIRST LIVING THING TO EXPLORE THE LAND

Figure 5. If that very first air-living plant had been cut by a sharp knife, this is a picture of the way it would have looked. See the little opening at the top which lets in the CO_2 and then on dry days closes to keep the chlorophyll from drying. After a drawing in *Evolution of the Plant Kingdom* by M. C. Coulter (*Nature of the World and of Man*).

the naked eye. The pores, too, cannot be seen. The picture shows the way the plant looks through a microscope.

It is a wonderful device, this, whereby the primitive plant can keep alive in the air and high 'up on the bank of the river. We should remember, however, that it took millions of years, and during that time millions of little seaweeds met with a terrible death; for they dried up and died like travelers lost in a desert. Fortunately all seaweeds were not alike. Those that had unfortunate shapes died by drying or suffocating. Only those that happened to have good shapes survived.

Even today it is fortunate that we are not all born exactly alike, for if we were all alike we should all want

If we all chose
to be doctors —

to do the same thing. As it is, some of us want to be doctors, some try to go to the South Pole, and some teach; so it has been very fortunate that for hundreds of millions of years little seaweeds, little fishes, little monkeys, and little children have not all been exactly alike.

Those groups of cells which clung to the rocks in the water still continued to live very peacefully. They took their food from the gases and mineral matter in the water and lived a quiet and happy life with their neighbors. Sometimes a powerful seaweed would crowd a weaker one just as we have seen a large tree shade the ground from the sun so thoroughly that small trees and plants cannot grow near it; thus we find a struggle for life even among the plants.

Some of the other groups of cells got food by fastening themselves to the rocks. Then the cells on the outer surface had the job of protecting the other cells from being hurt. Consequently these outer cells first grew tough, then hard, and finally, the wonderful coral was produced (Figure 6).

We have seen that the first great event after the earth became cool and blue sky appeared was the appearance in the water of the little germs that became bacteria, and the second important event was the uniting of the cells in groups so that the cells of each group could divide the work of living between them and help one another. Now a third great event took place. Those groups which floated in the water and eventually became jellyfish developed an appetite for some of the little single cells which hadn't joined any group. If there had been newspapers in those days, there would have been great headlines announcing that war had been declared by the groups against the individuals. Worse even than that, the individuals were being eaten alive by the groups. This was the very beginning of fighting and killing on the earth and of one animal's eating another. The habit of eating each other grew until finally one group of cells would eat smaller and weaker groups as well as individuals.

THE CELLS EAT EACH OTHER

Heretofore these little groups of cells had taken for food the gases that were dissolved in the water. Their only dangers had been the swift currents of the ocean and the hot lava which made the water boil. When. however.

Courtesy of the American Museum of Natural History

CORAL

Figure 6. The soft cells leave behind these hard skeletons called "coral." These groups of living cells live on top of each other as we do in cities, but unlike people in our cities they are deaf, dumb, and blind. From an exhibit in the American Museum of Natural History, New York, N. Y.

they began to eat each other, life became very dangerous. Yet we ought to be thankful that our ancestors did become cannibals, for the groups of cells developed more rapidly when they tried to catch the weaker groups or escape from the stronger ones. Thus the earth became full of fighting and killing and eating of one another and has remained so ever since. In general, animals don't eat their near relatives and very few human beings eat each other. Those that do we call cannibals.

Some of the groups happened to be able to move a little and to push themselves through the water. This gave them a tremendous advantage over those that couldn't, for they could go and get their food instead of waiting for it to float by, and also they could swim away from danger. Perhaps we ought not to call this feeble effort swimming, for they were just barely able to move at first and only went through the water when it was very calm. If there were waves thousands of these little groups would be killed because they couldn't swim fast enough to get out of the way. You see, therefore, that if one could wiggle his sides fast enough to move out of danger, he had a great advantage. He might live when all his companions were killed. If his children inherited his ability to wiggle, after a long time there would be a whole family of wigglers which could move away from a storm and could get their food more easily. Finally, such a group of cells grew into a jellyfish. Figure 7 is a picture of a jellyfish like those you can now find in the ocean. We know that they are almost exactly like the jellyfish that lived millions of years ago, for some of those ancient jellyfish got caught in the mud and turned into rock like the Montana bacteria. When these rocks are split open

[32]

JELLYFISH

Figure 7. This jellyfish wriggles through our oceans by flapping his sides as did his remote ancestor 500 million years ago. Photograph of an exhibit at the American Museum of Natural History, New York, N. Y.

we sometimes find the imprint of very ancient jellyfish.
Plants, fishes, and animals which have been turned into
rock after being in the ground for millions of years are
called fossils.

IV. SHELLS AND FISHES

AGAIN we must refer to those bluish-green little jellylike cells that are just visible in a microscope. You remember, some of these came together and formed little groups. Some of these groups floated close to the bottom of the shallow water near the shore. They seemed to get better food in this way than they could by attaching themselves to a rock or by floating near the surface. They kept close to the mud and sand where there wasn't much current in the water. To swim fast was no great advantage; however, they did need protection; for there was constant danger that they would be eaten alive by the creatures that could swim. Therefore if the cells on the outer layer happened to be tough, that group had a very considerable advantage and perhaps wouldn't be eaten by any other marauding group. The children of this group would inherit a tough skin. After thousands of years the advantage of having the protection of a tough skin became so great that the outer layer of cells became actually hard like a rock. We now call it a shell, and the little animals that are protected in this way we call shellfish. Some of these shellfish haven't changed very much even

[35]

down to the present time. In Figure 8 you will find two photographs of some shells. The one on the left is a fossil shell taken from rock that was formed about 500 million years ago. Those on the right are living shellfish with animals inside the shells. The animals have stretched

Courtesy of the American Museum of Natural History

LINGULELLA

Figure 8. A picture of a fossil lingulella on the left and a living successor on the right. Very little change in appearance has taken place in millions of years. From *Origin and Evolution of Life* by H. F. Osborn, published by Charles Scribner's Sons.

their long necks out from the shell probably in search of food. Clams and oysters were developed in this way.

Those groups of cells that floated very slowly near the bottom of the shallow parts of the sea didn't all become shellfish. Some developed a tough skin and long arms. They crawled very slowly on the sand and mud. We call some of these animals starfish. These starfish liked to eat the shellfish. It was hard for the starfish to do this unless the shellfish had his head out of his shell while he was hunting for food. Then if the starfish happened to be crawling very slowly over the sand and mud at that time he would grab the shellfish and eat him.

Once upon a time about 250 million years ago some starfish were attacking and trying to eat some shellfish, just as the starfish now try to eat oysters. But on that day of long ago a heavy mass of mud slid down on top of the starfish and shellfish that were fighting in the shallow sea and killed them all. Then the heat in the earth and the great weight of the rocks turned the mud and sand into rock. The starfish and the shellfish were turned into stone also. Lately the rock was found in New York State and split open, and there were the fossil starfish and shellfish just as they had been millions of years ago when that avalanche of mud prevented the starfish from eating the shellfish. Figure 9 is a photograph of that rock.

It seems strange that mud and sand can be turned into rock by merely pressing it and heating it. However, bricks are man-made rock, and they are made by molding clay into the shape of a brick and then heating it for a long time over a hot fire. If you take a handful of mud and squeeze it tight, you know, you can make it into a ball which will keep its shape for some time. Now the earth can squeeze a ball of mud as hard as if one of the wheels

STARFISH EATING SHELLFISH

Figure 9. In a place we now call Saugerties, New York, these starfish were eating shellfish in the far-off Devonian Period just as they eat oysters today, when they were suddenly covered with mud and later turned into stone. The shells are plainly visible among the starfish. From *Early Adaptation in the Feeding Habits of Starfishes* by John Mason Clarke, Director of the New York State Museum, Albany, N. Y.

of a railroad car were resting on it. It is hot far down in the earth, so that the mud is to some extent baked. Finally, instead of being squeezed for a few seconds like your mud ball, the earth keeps this mud baked and pressed for perhaps millions of years. No wonder mud and sand under such conditions are turned into rock.

This picture of the starfish shows that the shellfish were really in great danger. If any shellfish was born with a new shape which made it less likely to be eaten, it would have an advantage and be not so apt to meet with a tragic end. While these shellfish probably never changed very much, some new shellfish grew up from little groups of cells that had quite a different shape. The outer layers of the cell, which had to be tough in order to protect the group, developed into a spiral tube. Even today you can pick up shells like these on the beach at the seashore. Some of these little animals with spiral shells seem to have been prosperous, for they grew very long (Figure 10).

While some groups of cells were getting longer and narrower and swimming more rapidly through the water and while others were perishing because they happened to develop a poor shape for swimming, most of the groups stayed as they had been for millions of years. They could move just fast enough and get food enough to stay as groups, which somewhat resembled our jellyfish of today. For some unknown reason there was very little variation among their children, so that families of some round

SHELLFISH

Figure 10. A scene at low tide 500 million years ago. These straight shellfish were sometimes 15 feet long. That trilobite in the lower righthand corner of the picture will be grabbed and eaten by that shellfish if he isn't careful. From a mural painting by C. R. Knight in the Ernest R. Graham Hall, Field Museum of Natural History.

jellyfish stayed as round as their grandfathers from generation to generation even to the present time.

If you watch jellyfish in the ocean you will agree that if they were long and narrow they could go through the water more easily and could avoid being washed up on the beach in large numbers. If some jellyfish happened to be a little longer and narrower than the others they would have an advantage. They wouldn't be so apt to be driven up on the beach and destroyed by the waves. If their children also were a little narrower and longer they would be less likely to be killed. Then they could get their food better, for they could go after it instead of waiting for it to drift past them. On the other hand, if a jellyfish happened to grow with a shape that was worse than usual, it would have a hard time to get enough food, and if there were many of them with this bad shape, most of them would probably be killed by being driven on the rocks. The descendants of those that were left would also be hungry most of the time, and many of them, too, would be killed by the waves and by starvation. So after a while there wouldn't be any of these jellyfish with bad shapes left, and only jellyfish with good shapes would survive.

Certain of the descendants of these groups of cells, which somewhat resembled our modern jellyfish, changed a bit and then kept on changing. Some had a tougher outer skin and could swim faster. Apparently through millions of years those that developed a skin were less likely to get hurt, and their children were more likely to live. If they could swim faster they could get their food more easily, so that fewer of them would starve. After a long, long time there grew up a lot of little, long pointed fishes with real skins.

A few of the descendants of these early fishes have changed almost not at all. They are called lancelets

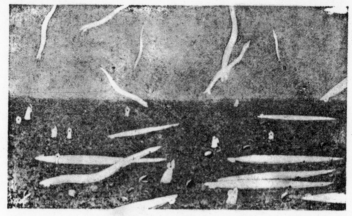

LANCELETS

Figure 11. These fishes live in the shallow water of the ocean. Their ancestors were much like them and were among the first fishes that were able to swim rapidly. From *Origin and Evolution of Life* by H. F. Osborn of the American Museum of Natural History.

(Figure 11). Being pointed at each end, they are good swimmers. Perhaps their ancestors were famous among their neighbors because for the first time in the world a skin had been developed behind which the owner could have some privacy. In order that this skin might be still tougher the fish developed scales. Lately a scientist at Princeton University discovered in the rocks of Vermont a fish's scale. The age of the rocks shows that the fish to which the scale belonged lived just after the little primitive fish had been developed. This Vermont fish is the oldest real fish with scales on its skin that has been found. It was probably small and perhaps not so handsome as some of our own fishes.

Not handsome? Tut, Tut!

V. MOUNTAINS AND RIVERS

WE HAVE been talking about the sea, but we haven't said a word about land and rivers and how these things came to exist. Why should some land project above the ocean and why should there be such a thing as a river? We want to know why some of the land is so steep and high that we call it a mountain. We must for a while leave our little germs and atoms of O and N and try to find out why the land rises above the waters and why the rivers flow into the ocean and why mountains rise up so high that their tops are covered with snow.

You remember that there were huge shooting stars falling on the earth and making it larger. Finally there were no more large stars left to fall; so the earth stopped growing. You remember also that these huge stars struck the earth with such tremendous force that the rock was melted. In this way the earth got a severe pounding. It was kneaded in much the way dough is kneaded when you make bread. Some parts of the earth are very heavy, for they are made of what we call lead and iron and other metals. Also some parts of the earth are lighter than iron, as, for example, ordinary rock. In the course of time—

millions of years—as the earth got well pounded and kneaded, many of the light parts like ordinary rock got forced to the surface and most of the heavy parts like iron sank down toward the center.

When the shooting stars stopped falling and the surface of the earth began to cool, some of these lighter parts which we call common rock made islands in the hot and forming crust. Perhaps after a while all these islands came together and formed one big piece which we call a continent. A German scientist thinks that they acted in this way, and some of the English and American scientists agree with him. You know bubbles on the water sometimes gather into one large cluster. In a way somewhat similar, these islands of rock came together and formed one large continent (Figure 12) which we call Pangea. It was a very large continent, for it was North and South America, Europe, Africa, Asia, and Australia all in one. For reasons we don't really know much about, this huge mass of land later separated into several pieces. Australia went off by itself and became a huge island in the southern Pacific Ocean. Then South America began to separate from Africa just as if it were a map that was being torn. This separation took tens of millions of years until finally North America, which was the last continent to draw away, had quite separated from Europe. Then for millions of years North and South America slowly, very slowly, slid toward the setting sun, until now the broad Atlantic Ocean lies between them and

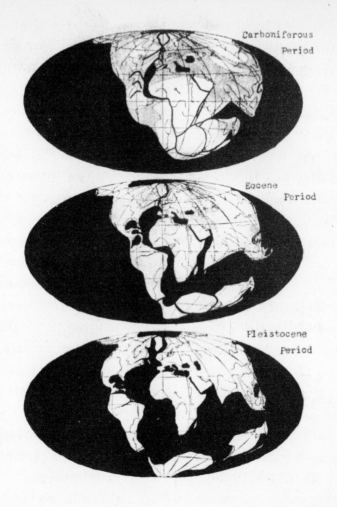

Carboniferous Period

Eocene Period

Pleistocene Period

MOVEMENT OF THE CONTINENTS

Figure 12. According to Alfred Wegener, a German scientist, there was but one large continent in the Carboniferous Period, and its name is Pangea. Finally it broke and the parts during millions of years slid to their present positions. The black areas represent deep water, the shaded areas shallow seas, and white represents land. After a drawing in *Origin of Continents and Oceans* by Alfred Wegener.

THE ORIGIN OF OCEANS AND RIVERS

Europe. If you look at a map of the world and imagine North and South America pushed up against Europe and Africa, you will see that the two great masses of land would fit together very nicely. No one really knows whether this did happen or not; so some of the scientists of the leading nations of the world are now measuring the distances from one continent to another just as carefully as they possibly can and hope in a few years to find out whether or not the continents are still moving apart.

You remember that when we began this story we found that the earth was so hot that all the water in the ocean was turned into steam and rose up in the sky in the form of dense clouds. Then torrents of rain fell down and even before they reached the earth were turned again into steam. Finally the earth cooled enough to form a crust, and when that got cold and hard the rain could stay on the earth without boiling and becoming steam. Then oceans grew in the hollow places and there was blue sky with only occasional storms.

The rain on these great continents that we have been describing settled into the hollow places and formed big pools of water which we now call ponds and lakes. After a while so much water poured into these lakes that they overflowed. The overflowing water then wore a channel all the way to the ocean. These channels we call rivers.

A river is constantly wearing away the land and carrying earth from its bottom and sides down to the ocean. You know how the rain during a thunderstorm cuts deep

[47]

ruts into soft ground that is not held firmly by grass, and you know how muddy the water is that flows off such ground. These little streams made by a thundershower behave just like rivers. They wear away the ground and carry it downstream. Sometimes a stream will flow into a pool of water. Then all the earth the stream is carrying is deposited in the pool of water close to where the stream entered. After a while the deposit is so big that it sticks out from the water and forms new land. In geography we call land made in this way a delta (Figure 13).

If a thunderstorm lasted all summer, you know that all the dirt that wasn't held firmly by grass, by roots of trees, and by rocks would be washed away and deposited far off where the brooks flow into some larger pond or where the rivers flow into the ocean.

This wearing away of the higher land and the forming of new land at the edge of the ocean is going on all the time, even if we don't have thundershowers all summer long; for the water is always carrying little particles of soil from the high land to the low land and eventually to the seashore.

You may think that after a while all the soil would be washed away and only rock would be left and then there would be nothing more to be deposited at the seashore. That would be true if it weren't that the rock that is exposed to the air is always slowly turning into small particles of soil. The next time you see a place where a road has been cut through a hill of solid rock you will probably see that the rock at the bottom of this cut near the road is solid and not cracked, while the rock near the top of the cut is cracked and sometimes merges into the

Courtesy of the U. S. Geological Survey

DELTA OF THE YAHTSE RIVER, ALASKA

Figure 13. This is a picture of the mouth of the river. The Pacific Ocean is in the distance. The river has deposited the gravel and pebbles that it has brought down from the mountains and formed this delta. After a photograph by I. C. Russell, U. S. Geological Survey.

soil so gradually that you can hardly tell where the soil begins and the rock leaves off. The picture, Figure 14, shows how soil is formed in this way. This is partly due to our old friends the atoms of O, for this gas attacks the rock and makes it crumble just like dead wood. Then

ROCK THAT IS BECOMING SOIL

Figure 14. This cut in the earth shows what is going on underneath the trees
and bushes. By the action of water and air the rock crumbles and
becomes soil. After G. P. Merril, U. S. National Museum.

the rain comes and washes these newly formed particles of dirt down into the valleys, and the rivers carry some of it to the seashore.

A WITHERED APPLE

Figure 15. As the moist body of this apple gradually dried, it became smaller. Since the skin could not become smaller, it had to wrinkle. When the inside of the earth slowly cools, the earth grows smaller. Since the earth's crust cannot grow smaller, it wrinkles and makes mountains. After a drawing in *New Astronomy* by S. P. Langley.

While all this is going on another great thing is happening: the earth is continuing to cool, and as it cools it grows a little smaller. Perhaps, also, it is growing smaller, very slowly, because deep down near the center of the earth the little atoms of rock are getting closer and closer

[51]

together. The crust of rock on which the oceans rest and on which the great island continents of light rock rest cannot get much smaller than it now is, for it has already nearly cooled off. Consequently this crust of the earth is bound to wrinkle. It wrinkles for about the same reason that a dried apple wrinkles. Figure 15 is a picture of an apple that has become a little smaller because it has dried up somewhat. The apple skin, however, was nearly dry in the beginning and so could not become much smaller; so there was too much skin for the apple. The result was that the skin had to form wrinkles, for the same reason that when a coat is too large for you it hangs in folds. These wrinkles usually come at the weakest places, for at such places the bending of the skin or crust is easiest.

The weakest places in the crust of the earth were sometimes near the seashore and sometimes where mud had been deposited at the bottom of inland seas for millions of years.

Since the inland seas and the shores are weak places, the crust of the earth began to fold at these points, and these folds we call mountains. In the course of millions of years huge mountains rose where once there had been only water. Figure 16 is a picture of some wrinkles in the layers of rock. Figure 17 is a model of the way some of these wrinkles in the crust of the earth would look if you were a giant and could cut a slice right out of the earth.

LOW HILLS AND SLUGGISH STREAMS

During all this time there were frequent storms, as there are now. Rain fell on the mountains and drained off into little brooks and then into rivers and finally into the ocean. Just as before, the water carried off every loose particle of sand and soil that it could get hold of. Grad-

Courtesy of the U. S. Geological Survey

MOUNT HEAVENS, MONTANA

Figure 16. Where the earth's crust has been wrinkled and folded. Heavens Fold near Heavens Peak, Montana. Photographed by the U. S. Geological Survey.

ually through millions of years these mountains were worn down, smoothed over, and thus made much lower and smaller. Then instead of mountain torrents plunging in a series of cascades down steep slopes into the valleys, there were sluggish streams which very slowly flowed down low hills, or through long plains into the ocean (Figure 18).

[53]

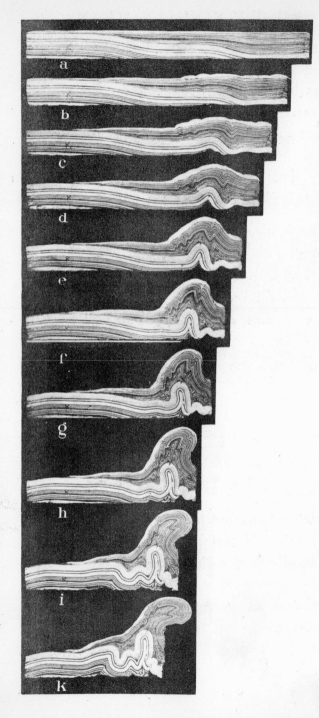

HOW WRINKLES IN THE EARTH'S CRUST ARE MADE

Figure 17. Experiments imitating the folds found in mountain ranges. A photograph of models made by Bailey Willis, U. S. Geological Survey.

BUT THE CRUST WRINKLES AGAIN

But still mud and sand were deposited, layer after layer, along the edges of the great land masses and sank by their own weight deep down into the crust of the earth, where they were baked and pressed into rock. Always the earth kept on growing a little smaller. Always the crust,

Courtesy of the U. S. Geological Survey

A SLUGGISH STREAM

Figure 18. Little by little this meandering river digs away the high bank and widens the valley. Trout Creek, Yellowstone National Park. After a photograph by C. D. Walcott, U. S. Geological Survey.

which couldn't grow any smaller, had to fold and wrinkle in its weakest places, and these places were usually where the layers of mud and sand had sunk deep down into the earth.

Probably we ought not to say that the making of mountains has been always going on. Although the earth was continually cooling there would be times when it hadn't shrunk enough to make the crust wrinkle. Then again there would be other times when the crust would wrinkle a great deal and would catch up with the slowly shrinking earth. So there have been formed successive mountain ranges. Sometimes new wrinkles will form in the very places where old wrinkles have been worn away. Once upon a time, where Massachusetts and Connecticut now are, great wrinkles were formed. After millions of years these mountains were all worn away by rain and snow. Then a new wrinkle came, the land rose several hundred feet, and once more the rivers started on their long, tedious wearing away of the land and carrying the soil particles down to the seashore. They are still patiently doing it. The Connecticut River has cut out for itself a broad valley so that you would hardly believe as you cross it now that it once rushed into Long Island Sound between high cliffs which it had cut from the rock. Of course this land did not rise in a few days or in a few centuries. It possibly took thousands of years to rise, but even so, it rose faster than the river could wear it away.

The way a stream cuts first a deep canyon and then a broad valley is very interesting. As we said before, when a stream after a thundershower is cutting its way through soft ground it makes a little canyon, for the channel is narrow and the sides almost perpendicular. To an insect it would be a deep chasm through the bottom of which a mountain torrent was rushing. If you watch this stream for a few minutes you will find that it is cutting away the dirt from the bottom of the insect's cliffs. This is called undermining the sides of the cliffs. Soon large sections of the sides begin to fall into the stream. It is possible to watch such a little rivulet make a wider and wider valley through the soft ground. Mountain rivers behave in just this way. While a little stream caused by a thunder shower cuts a wide canyon in a few minutes through the soft earth, a mountain river will take thousands of years to cut a broad canyon through solid rock (Figure 19).

When the canyon becomes broad and the sides merely smooth sloping hills, the wearing away of the rock and the further widening of the valley becomes more difficult; for the stream now moves more slowly because it has worn away the high land that had made it a torrent. It has widened its valley until it flows through a level plain of considerable extent. Then the river wanders over this plain, but every now and then it will wear a channel close to the side of the valley. In this way it digs a little more from the sides of the hills, and so gradually, very slowly, the valley is widened. This wandering of the river is called meandering (Figure 18).

The sharp curves in the stream are constantly changing their positions, for the water eats away the bank on the outer edge and deposits earth on the inner edge. These sharp curves slowly travel down the valley. As they move they are always carrying away part of the higher land on

A YOUNG RIVER

Figure 19. This river has cut a deep channel, but it has not had time to make
a broad valley. Grand Canyon of the Yellowstone River, Yellowstone
National Park.

PENEPLANES

each side of the broad valley. In thousands and sometimes millions of years the brooks, the mountain torrents,
and the meandering streams will carry away all the

Courtesy of the U. S. Geological Survey

SLOWLY THIS MIGHTY MOUNTAIN IS DISAPPEARING

Figure 20. The air, assisted by rain and snow, is wearing this mountain down.
The long sloping masses of broken and fallen rock look like snow drifts.
Mt. Sneppels, Colorado. After a photograph by W. Cross, U. S.
Geological Survey.

mountains and hills and leave the country almost a level
plain, which is called a peneplane, because "pene" in
Latin means "almost."

Mountains that are old have been worn into smooth

WHY MOUNTAINS WEAR AWAY

Figure 21. Slowly this ledge of rock is falling in pieces. Nevada City, California. After a photograph by G. K. Gilbert, U. S. Geological Survey.

shapes and are not so very high. As a rule they have very few precipices or deep gorges and canyons, for all these rough edges have been worn away. On the other hand, newly formed wrinkles or mountains are usually very

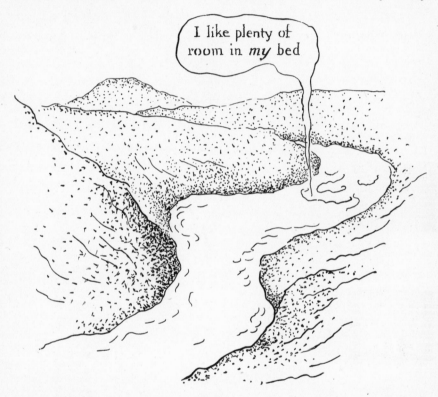

high and full of sharp peaks and steep sides and deep canyons through which, sometimes, mountain torrents are rushing. The new mountains are just like the soft ground after a thunder storm. They are full of sharp edges and cliffs. After millions of years the river in the canyon cuts out a broad valley and the sharp peaks of the mountains are worn into rounded hills.

The Appalachian Mountains are very old and have become well rounded and covered with bushes and trees. The Rocky Mountains, on the other hand, are a much newer range. Figure 20 gives some idea of the way they are being cut away by wind and rain.

The picture, Figure 21, shows just how some mountains are worn away. These thin slabs of rock, loosened by rain and the gases in the air, are broken away from the cliff because the rock expands in the hot sunlight and contracts when it is cold at night. Nearly everything grows a little larger when it is hot and shrinks a little when it is cold, and these great ledges of rock are no exception. Even though this movement of the rock is very, very small, it is enough to break off large slabs. Stone Mountain, near Atlanta, Georgia, has been rounded off in this manner.

VI. VOLCANOES

SOMETIMES as the crust of the earth has wrinkled and jammed by the slow cooling and shrinking of the earth, cracks have been made in the rocks and then the hot melted rock from far down in the earth has come out and flowed over the land like molasses. We call melted rock that bubbles up from inside the earth *lava*. Sometimes the crack in the earth is shaped more or less like a round hole, and when the lava comes out it spreads all around that hole and cools into rock. Some time later more lava comes and flows over the mound and makes it higher. After a long, long time the mound grows into a mountain which we call a volcano. The hole in the center through which the hot melted lava occasionally comes is called the crater. Sometimes the lava is actually hot enough to boil in the crater, and then great masses of gas, steam and smoke come out from the top of the volcano. Figure 22 is a picture of a volcano. Occasionally melted rock, or lava as we call it, not only flows down the side of a mountain but keeps on flowing over the land below and burying everything that is in its path.

When a city is near a volcano it is always in danger of

being buried some day by a great mass of lava that may flow down the sides of the mountain. Nearly 2,000 years ago there was a city in Italy named Pompeii which got buried in this way. Many Romans lived in this city,

Courtesy of B. F. Loomis

LASSEN PEAK, CALIFORNIA

Figure 22. Eruption of Sept. 5, 1924. In the left side of the picture one can clearly see the great masses of ashes falling from the smoke cloud. "When a mighty mountain speaks, even in a whisper, the whole world sits up and listens." From *Pictorial History of the Lassen Volcano* by B. F. Loomis.

and many of them were killed when the city was buried. During the last hundred years the Italians have dug away the ashes and lava and dirt that covered Pompeii so that now we can study the ruins of houses 2,000 years old and can understand how people lived in that long-ago

POMPEII

Figure 23. Upper picture: Pompeii before the eruption of Vesuvius. The central building is the Temple of Jupiter. Lower picture: the condition of the city and temple today. After a drawing in *Wonders of the Past* by **J. A.** Hammerton.

time. Figure 23 is a picture of the ruins as they are today; it also shows how the city looked when the Romans lived there. Even a volcanic eruption is very useful sometimes, for, you see, it can tell us by burying and so preserving a city how people lived long ago. It was unfortunate for the Romans who got caught in the streets of Pompeii and were killed, but tens of thousands of people have been killed by volcanoes in many parts of the world in all ages since man has been on this earth.

There is a great park out in the Rocky Mountains called the Yellowstone National Park. The Yellowstone River has been flowing through this part of the country for millions of years, so that it has had time to wear away a deep channel (Figure 19). The sides of this channel are still steep, for even in thousands of years it hasn't had time to wear away the sides and carry their mud and sand to the ocean. These cliffs on the banks of the river show what happened in this part of the continent millions of years ago, for near the bottom of the cliff you will find buried the stumps of huge trees that have been turned into stone (Figure 24). They are called petrified trees or petrified wood. A long time ago there was a great forest where these petrified stumps are now buried. Then there was a volcanic eruption of ashes (Figure 25) which covered the forest and turned the stumps of the trees to stone.

After a very long time the rain and the atoms of O in

A FOSSIL TREE OF THE LAST FOREST TO BE BURIED

Figure 24. Millions of years ago this fossil tree was part of a luxuriant forest. Under it lie fourteen buried forests. Once more and perhaps for the last time the great volcanoes which surrounded what is now Yellowstone National Park threw out masses of ashes and pumice stone and the last, the fourteenth forest, was buried. Now the rain and the Yellowstone River have worn away the ashes that have been turned into rock, and this tree trunk, now a fossil, once more stands erect in the sunlight. From "Standing Stone Forests of Wyoming" by G. E. Mitchell (*Scientific American*, February, 1926).

the air turned some of these ashes into little particles of soil. Then seeds blew in and sprouted. Finally a whole new forest grew on top of that layer of old petrified stumps.

But the most remarkable thing about that cliff on the

MOUNT PELEE

Figure 25. Dust or ashes falling upon the land after being blown from the volcano, Mt. Pelee. After a painting by C. R. Knight.

banks of the Yellowstone River is that as you climb up from the bottom you will find fifteen layers of these petrified forests (Figure 26). Fifteen times a great forest had grown in this spot, and fifteen times it had been overwhelmed by ashes from volcanic outbursts. Think how long it must have taken for each forest to grow! Fifteen times that catastrophe happened, and fifteen times ages

FIFTEEN BURIED FOSSIL FORESTS

Figure 26. If a giant with a huge knife cut through the sides of the canyon of the Yellowstone River, this is a picture of what you would see. The lowest layer of fossil trunks was a green forest perhaps 19 million years ago. It may have taken millions of years to grow and bury the fifteen forests. From "Standing Forests of Wyoming," by G. E. Mitchell (*Scientific American*, February, 1926).

were used in making a new forest. This is another example both of the tremendous age of the earth and also of how much we can learn from buried cities, forests, and fossils.

Thus the earth is always changing. *Our Mobile Earth* was a name well chosen by R. A. Daly when he wrote his book on mountains, earthquakes, and continents, for "mobile" means "easily changing." Later you will learn about some of the tremendous effects these changes had on the ancestors of all living creatures.

Never annoy a volcano.

VII. SILURIAN PERIOD

THE time when the little germs became cells and the groups of cells became jellyfish was so long ago that we might say it was at the very dawn of the history of life on this earth. For hundreds of millions of years changes in fishes and seaweeds took place very slowly. It would hardly have been necessary to have a calendar in those days, for one year followed another in a monotonous and endless succession. However when the sea became crowded and the plants and animals began to explore the land, some queer things happened and the history of the earth became more exciting. From this time on we will give a name to each great period of time.

You know how we measure our own history in years; that is, we say we are ten or fifteen years old. The history of America is so long that we sometimes give a name to a whole group of years; we speak, for example, of the Colonial Period, which was more than a hundred years long. Also we read about the times of the Greeks or the Romans, and each one of these periods was several hundred years long. The Egyptians were a wonderful people, and the Egyptian Period lasted for several thousand

years. Therefore, when we want to describe a long time
we are accustomed to give a name to a group of years.
In the same way the history of the earth has been divided
into periods, but the time of each of these periods is enor-
mously long—so long that the Egyptian Period seems
but a moment in comparison. To some extent we are prepared for long periods in the history of the earth, for you
remember those fifteen fossil forests in the Yellowstone
National Park and the ages it must have taken to grow a
forest of huge trees fifteen times in succession. Therefore you will not be surprised to learn that the periods
in the earth's history are always measured in millions of
years.

The period when the land began to be covered with
plants and when the fishes first came out of the water
to live on land is called the Silurian Period. We think it
began 390 million years ago and lasted forty million
years.

All forms of life are described by two names, "flora"
and "fauna." Trees, plants, seaweed, and grass are called
flora, and fauna is the name for all other kinds of life such
as fishes, clams, insects, birds, and human beings. The
flora were the first forms of life to explore the dry land
and to learn how to live in the air (Figure 27). In this
Silurian Period some of the fauna were crowded out of
the water and tried living for at least a part of the time
on the land. Scorpions were the pioneers. They were not

Courtesy of the Field Museum of Natural History

THE SHORES OF NORTH AMERICA IN THE SILURIAN PERIOD

Figure 27. The Silurian seaweed is lying in the sun on masses of coral. From a painting by Charles R. Knight in the Ernest R. Graham Hall, Field Museum of Natural History.

our ancestòrs, however, for having become scorpions and having learned to live on the land, they were apparently satisfied with themselves, for they have stayed scorpions ever since. They, therefore, among the fauna, have the longest family tree of air-breathing ancestors.

Apparently the scorpions are descended from a jointed sea worm with thick tough skin such as beetles now have. These worms may in their turn have descended from something very much like an elongated jellyfish which happened to develop into a tough-skinned, slow-moving worm.

This worm developed a pair of legs for each of several joints in its body, and then after millions of years it became a scorpion, but still continued to live under water (Figure 28). The sea scorpions seem to have been very efficient both in defending themselves and in getting food, and soon became enormous creatures; some fossil sea scorpions of this period have been found in New York State that were three feet long. Figure 29 is a picture of one of these monsters.

Some of the small sea scorpions probably had a hard time to get enough food and at the same time not be killed and eaten by the big scorpions and fishes. They evidently kept in shallow water and were therefore frequently left at low tide in mud puddles on the flats. Possibly the earth's crust wrinkled a little at this time, so that many shallow seas very slowly became mud flats.

LIFE IN A SHALLOW SEA IN THE SILURIAN PERIOD

Figure 28. Those large creatures are sea-scorpions. Some trilobites are in the lower lefthand corner. In the lower righthand corner a king-crab is crawling toward the trilobites. Drawn by Alice B. Woodward in *Nebula to Man* by Henry R. Knipe, published by J. M. Dent and Company, London.   *Courtesy of Miss Alice B. Woodward*

In this way some learned to get the atoms of O that they needed directly from the air. Their thick skin kept them from drying up when they were exposed to the sunlight, for fauna, like flora, must keep moist or they will die. Nearly all animals, including ourselves, must drink water very frequently or they would die of thirst.

In adapting themselves to air and sunlight the scorpions must have suffered as many tragic experiences as the plants. Millions of scorpions probably perished before a type appeared that didn't have to go back to the ocean at high water in order to keep from drying up and dying. Fortunately for us, land scorpions were small in comparison with some of their cousins in the sea, and they have remained small even to the present time (Figure 30). Figure 31 is a picture of one of these scorpions that became a fossil and was found in the rocks of Scotland. Some of these were two and a half inches long.

Millions of years after the scorpions came out of the sea, centipedes crawled from the mud flats and learned to enjoy breathing the air and climbing over the rocks. They, too, were descended from those same sea worms that were the ancestors of the scorpions. They haven't changed much in the several hundred million years during which they have been living on dry land.

The plants of the Silurian Period were very simple and much like that seaweed that first tried to live on land. These plants were less than a foot high. Their roots were very weak and were used mostly for drawing water from

GIANT SEA SCORPION

Figure 29. The fossil remains of this crustacean were found near Buffalo, New York. His name is Stylonurus and he was three feet long. From an exhibit in the New York State Museum, Albany, New York.

the ground—not, as roots are today, for holding the plant erect as well as for drawing water. Perhaps it was due

Courtesy of the American Museum of Natural History

SCORPION OF TODAY

Figure 30. This is a picture of one of our own living scorpions. He lives by eating insects and hunts by night. The sting is at the end of the tail. From an exhibit in the American Museum of Natural History.

to their weak roots that the plants were so small, for if one had grown tall it surely would have been blown over and killed.

A SILURIAN MAP

Now that life has come out of the ocean and some plants, scorpions, and centipedes are living on the land,

PALAEOPTERNUS

Figure 31. A picture of a fossil scorpion which lived in Scotland during the Silurian Period. His bold ancestors were the first of the fauna to rise from the sea and explore the land. From *Geology* by Joseph Le Conte of the University of California.

we should think about a map and try to draw a picture of the way North America looked in those days. Perhaps North America in the Silurian Period was lying alongside of Europe or, perhaps, it was lying just where it is today; as we have said before, we do not know the answer. We do know that, whether it was anchored near Europe or sliding on its way to the Pacific Ocean, it was the same old North America that we know so well, except that the shore extended farther out to sea. Until we learn differently we will assume hereafter that North America has always been by itself and has always had an ocean on each side.

Compared with our modern map North America had a very queer shape in the Silurian Period. In Figure 32 the Silurian map is drawn on the same sheet with the present map, so that you can see just how the shape of the continent has changed. You will notice that in those very ancient days there were no Great Lakes. Hudson Bay is missing from the Silurian map. The Gulf of Mexico is a long, narrow channel that starts in the Pacific Ocean and extends over part of Mexico, Mississippi, Kentucky, New York, the southern part of Labrador, and the northern part of Newfoundland.

This long, narrow sea is very interesting, for streams and rivers kept wearing away the land on each side and filling this sea with mud and sand. Finally, this mud and sand, sinking deep down into the crust of the earth, became one of the weak spots, and when the earth shrank again by cooling, wrinkles were formed where the sea had been. These wrinkles we call the Appalachian Mountains. However, they didn't come until a long time after the Silurian and several other periods had passed.

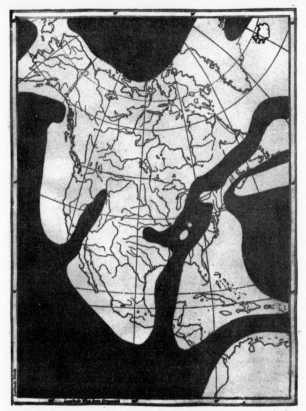

MAP OF NORTH AMERICA IN THE SILURIAN PERIOD

Figure 32. After a map in *Historical Geology* by Charles Schuchert of Yale University, published by John Wiley and Sons, Inc. An outline map by Rand McNally and Company of North America at the present time has been placed over the Silurian map in order to show how the outlines of the continent in the Silurian Period differed from those of today.

Besides helping to make mountains, these shallow seas did some other useful things for the earth; they gave us our great beds of salt. Sometimes the seas were so shallow that they would evaporate in hot sunlight and leave only dry land. Of course any salt that was in the water was left on the land.

When water disappears into the air in this way it is said to evaporate. You can illustrate this by filling a dish with salt water and letting it stand for a few days. It will evaporate, and you will find all the salt that you had dissolved in the water left on the dish in the form of a very thin coating. If without removing the salt you fill the dish again and again with salt water and each time allow the water to evaporate, you will find that the coating of salt in the dish grows deeper and deeper. If you keep evaporating the salt water for a long enough time you will have a thick layer of salt in the dish.

Some of these shallow seas behaved just like a dish of salt water. For millions of years they were alternately dry land and then shallow sea, until the layer of salt at the bottom became sometimes several hundred feet thick. During the Silurian Period such a sea existed over a large part of the State of New York. After the salt had been spread over hundreds of square miles, it was covered with sand and mud. Now these beds of salt are mined and provide you with most of the salt that you eat.

Such a bed of salt may some day be formed near Salt Lake City in the State of Utah. You have probably heard how very salt the water is in the Great Salt Lake, which was, many thousands of years ago, much larger than it is today. It has gradually dried up until now only a small and shallow lake is left. If this lake should dry up completely, it would leave a thick layer of salt.

You remember that in the beginning, when the little bacteria first appeared, the ocean wasn't at all salty. When this lake in Utah was large and covered part of the States of Nevada, Colorado, and Utah its water was fresh. We say water is fresh when it is good to drink; however, even such water contains just a trace of salt, but so little that you cannot taste it. All the springs, brooks and rivers dissolve out of the rocks and soil some of the little particles that we call salt. Most of these atoms are carried into the ocean, and there they stay forever. This is because the ocean behaves like the salt water in that dish. When the sun evaporates the water of the ocean and forms clouds the salt is left behind. Then the rain falls from the clouds and soaks into the land and forms springs which dissolve from the ground more of the little salt particles. The sea, therefore, acts like a huge mouse-trap. It catches all the little particles of salt and lets none escape. You are probably thinking that the ocean is growing more salty all the time, and that is exactly the truth. It is growing more salty so slowly, however, that even Columbus, if he came back to the earth, would notice no difference.

This lake that thousands of years ago covered so much of the State of Utah has been named Lake Bonneville.

It behaved in a small way just like the ocean. All the brooks and rivers that flowed into Lake Bonneville carried tiny particles of salt. When the sun, however, evaporated the water and formed clouds, the salt was left in the lake. Finally a dry period came and the water evaporated much faster than it could be supplied by the streams. Now a much smaller and very salty lake is left which we call Great Salt Lake. Figure 33 is a picture of the old beaches that were made by the waves of Lake Bonneville. Now of course they are high and dry on the sides of the hills.

If the water in a lake can flow into the ocean, the lake remains fresh and good to drink, because the water in it is then being constantly changed. The old water flows out, and new water from the streams takes its place. Although this water contains a few particles of salt, we cannot taste them, and so we call the water fresh.

It is very different when the country is dry and hot so that the water in a lake is evaporated as fast as new water can flow into it from streams and rivers. Then the little particles of salt cannot flow away to the ocean. They are caught in the trap and cannot escape. Each day more and more are brought to the lake by streams and brooks until after thousands of years the lake becomes so full of little particles of salt that it is not good to drink and we call it a salt lake (Figure 34). Then if a dry period comes and the streams stop flowing, the lake gradually becomes dry

[84]

THE OLD BEACHES OF LAKE BONNEVILLE

Figure 33. These dry beaches on the side of the hill were cut by the waves of Lake Bonneville when the water was 1,000 feet deep over this part of the country. From the frontispiece of the monograph *The Old Beaches of Lake Bonneville* by G. K. Gilbert of the U. S. Geological Survey.

and the great accumulation of salt particles is left as a white crust on the land.

Sometimes dust and sand are blown over this layer of salt, and sometimes the basin where the lake used to be is again filled with water—perhaps a part of an inland sea. Mud is then deposited on top of the sand and dust until

Courtesy of the U. S. Geological Survey

A SALT LAKE

Figure 34. The shores of a salt lake photographed by the U. S. Geological Survey.

finally the layer of salt is buried deep in the earth. If this sea later disappears we can dig into these great beds and cut out tons of rock salt which we grind into the fine white powder that we use in our food. Figure 35 is a picture of a large room that has been cut from the solid salt

in a mine in Poland. Men have been cutting salt from
this mine for 2,000 years. Lately a salt mine used by the

Courtesy of Sir Isaac Pitman and Sons, Ltd.

A SALT MINE

Figure 35. This famous mine at Slanicu in Roumania has been worked since
the time of the Romans. From a drawing in *Salt* by A. F. Calvert.

ancient Indians of America about 2,000 years ago was
discovered in Nevada. Figure 36 is a picture of this old

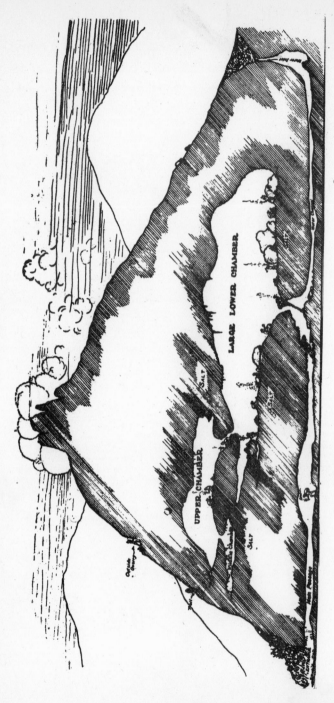

A CROSS-SECTION OF A VERY OLD INDIAN SALT MINE

Figure 36. Perhaps 3,000 years ago Indians began to dig salt from this hill. When recently explored many stone hammers and sandals were found. There were also corn-cobs left from ancient lunches. This old salt mine is 6 miles south of St. Thomas, Nevada. From "Ancient Salt Mines of the Indians," by M. R. Harrington of the Museum of the American Indian (*Scientific American*, August, 1926).

mine. When the mine was discovered many of the tools used by the ancient Indians were found. Explorers even found partly eaten ears of corn that perhaps had been taken into the mine for a noonday lunch.

"Say, Scorpy, what does SILURIAN mean?"

VIII. DEVONIAN PERIOD

THE next period is called Devonian. It began about 350 million years ago when the Silurian Period ended, and lasted fifty million years. It is a very important period in our family history, for it was during this fifty million years that some animals that later became our ancestors came out of the sea and started their long career on the land. They are called amphibians, for they lived part of the time in the sea and part of the time on land. Frogs of today are also amphibians. Like Robinson Crusoe's good man Friday, this amphibian ancestor made himself known by leaving his footprint, not on Crusoe's Island, but on the rocks of Pennsylvania. Figure 37 is a picture of this fossil footprint. The old fellow may have looked much like the picture in Figure 39. Because some of the fossils of later generations have been found in rocks, and for various other reasons, it has been possible to draw a picture that gives some idea of the way this early ancestor appeared. His name is Thinopus.

Like the scorpions and centipedes of the Silurian Period, many of the fishes probably preferred shallow water, where they were less likely to be attacked by the big fish and where they in their turn could kill and eat the still smaller fish.

The shallow water had another danger for these fishes —the danger of being stranded at ebb tide. Many fishes

Courtesy of the Peabody Museum of Yale University

A FOOTPRINT OF THINOPUS

Figure 37. The earliest known footprint. It was made by Thinopus when he crawled over a mud flat in Pennsylvania in the Devonian Period. It is now preserved in the Peabody Museum of Yale University.

must have suffocated in the air on those occasions, for they couldn't breathe without water. Their fins made very poor legs with which to crawl back into the ocean. You can see what a great advantage a fish would have if he could use his fins to help him flop toward the water

(Figure 38). He would be much more apt to survive. Since fishes are not all just alike, some did have fins that helped them to crawl. Their children inherited fins of this shape. Also the fins of the children were not all just

THE JUMPING FISH, PERIOPHTHALMUS

Figure 38. This fish, now found in the tropics, perhaps illustrates crudely the way in which our ancestors changed a fin into a foot. He flops over the mud flats with considerable speed, but he has never developed feet as our amphibian ancestors did. From a drawing by F. A. Lucas in *Two Years in the Jungle*, by William T. Hornaday, copyright 1885 by Charles Scribner's Sons.

alike. Those fish-children which happened to have fins more suitable for crawling had a still better chance to escape drying and dying on the flats at low tide. Also it may be that the continents rose a little as the shrinking earth made the crust squirm and heave. Then the inland seas, perhaps, became shallow until only mud flats and small pools remained. The fish caught in this manner must breathe air part of the time or die. Of course these changes took millions of years. So gradually a fish's fin became a foot.

The slow development of a fin into a foot is illustrated in Figure 39. The fin became a flapper or a paddle, and then the paddle became a foot. At first the fin was merely a tough fold in the fish's skin. As the skeleton developed, the muscles of the fin turned into fine bones. You can see these bones in Figure 39-A. In B, the bones became larger. Finally in C, the "foot stage," five toes were developed. This is the origin of our five toes on each foot or five fingers on each hand. It was only a few million years ago that we first stood erect and used our forelegs as "arms" with five fingers at the end of each arm. During nearly all the 300 million years since our ancestor the fish developed a foot, our family has moved around on four feet, and each foot has had the five toes which that ancestral fish found so convenient when he wished to get back into the water. Perhaps there was a period when our amphibian ancestors had one big toe and two rather clumsy smaller toes on each foot, and then they later developed the familiar five toes.

Just as the scorpions learned to get atoms of O from the air instead of from the water, so the fishes, while they were flapping around and developing five-toed feet, also

ARTHRODIRA

Figure 40. This gigantic Devonian fish was eight feet long and lived where the city of Cleveland now is. After a model by Dr. Hussakof and Mr. Horter in the American Museum of Natural History.

learned how to breathe air. For many millions of years, however, the descendants of Thinopus lived part of the

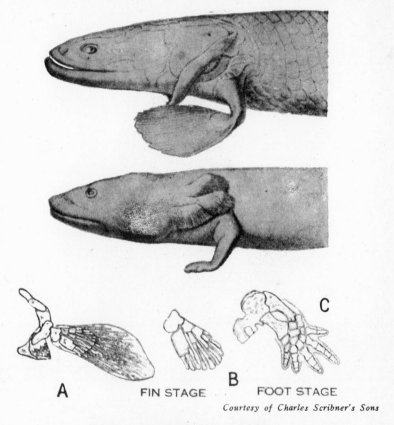

FIN STAGE   FOOT STAGE

Courtesy of Charles Scribner's Sons

HOW A FIN BECAME A FOOT

Figure 39. The development of a foot from a fin. After a drawing by Klaatsch. From *Origin and Evolution of Life* by H. F. Osborn of the American Museum of Natural History.

time in the sea, walking on shore and breathing the air only at low tide when they were hunting for stranded fish that couldn't crawl back to the sea.

DEVONIAN SPONGES AND SEAWEED

Figure 41. From the shallow Devonian seas which once covered Cattaraugus County, New York. From a photograph of an exhibit at the New York State Museum at Albany.

DEVONIAN SHARKS

If you look at the picture of an Arthrodira (Figure 40) you will realize why some of the smaller fish preferred to live in shallow water. These large fossil Devonian fish are found in the rocks near Cleveland, Ohio, and also in Germany; many of them were sharks about five feet long, and huge sea scorpions of the Silurian Period were still numerous in those Devonian waters. So some small fish were wise enough to keep close to the shore, where, however, many perished when the tide left them stranded; but others learned to become amphibians and were the ancestors of mankind.

Life on the bottom of the ocean, where the water wasn't too deep, had become very interesting during this period. Many sponges and corals had developed. Some of these became fossils and have been found near Olean in the State of New York. They are now reproduced in the New York State Museum at Albany. Figure 41 is a picture of this exhibit. The seaweeds grew tall and had fantastic shapes. Also the shellfish in some cases became so strong that they could catch and eat small, slow-moving fish. These little, sluggish fish got some protection by developing a thick, hard skin like armor. Our crabs and lobsters are built this way even today. However, this means of protection was only partially successful, as you can see by looking at the picture in Figure 42, where a large shellfish is shown eating a small armored fish. Some of these small slow-moving fish would have perished entirely and become extinct if it had not been for

TRILOBITE

Figure 42. Devonian shellfish eating a small armored fish called a trilobite. After a restoration of Devonian marine life at the New York State Museum at Albany.

their very large families. More were born than could possibly be killed by their enemies, and so they kept their family name in the ocean for many generations.

If there had been social life among the early dwellers of the sea, trilobite would have been a very common name. From early times trilobites had crawled over the bottom of the shallow seas. Finally their enemies became too powerful, and they ceased to exist. The small crustacean that is being eaten alive by a large shellfish in Figure 42 is a trilobite. Figure 43 shows the way a trilobite looked, for many of them have been found fossilized in the rocks.

It is hard to tell why this ancient and large family met with so hard a fate. That they were very old-fashioned and didn't change their way of living to suit new conditions couldn't have been the reason, because we find horseshoe crabs that are very much like those of today (Figure 44). If a horseshoe crab could survive, you would think that a trilobite could, but the fact is that he did not.

Another way in which these small armored fish could perish is illustrated in Figures 45 and 46. These little fishes are called Bothriolepi. They were first cousins of Arthrodira, that savage fish with enormous mouth. It was in the latter part of the Devonian Period that a group of these little Bothriolepi in Canada were swimming upstream one day in search of food when they were suddenly buried by a landslide of mud. It overwhelmed them so quickly that they couldn't even move. Then more mud covered them until they were so deep down in the earth that they were finally baked and pressed into rock.

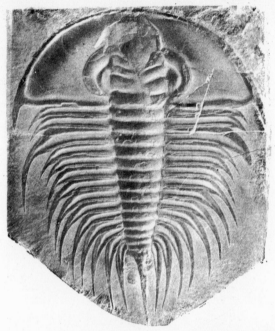

Courtesy U. S. National Museum

A VERY ANCIENT TRILOBITE

Figure 43. This trilobite some 550 million years ago lived at a place we now call Georgia, Vermont. He got into the mud which was later pressed and baked into rock and which is now Parker's quarry. As a fossil this trilobite lives at the U. S. National Museum at Washington. From *Cambrian Geology and Palaeontology* by C. D. Walcott, U. S. Geological Survey (Smithsonian Miscellaneous Collections).

Millions of years afterward, the earth wrinkled at this place and the rock containing these fossils was raised. Then rain and streams wore away enough of the rock to uncover them. Finally a scientist found them there and placed them in a museum.

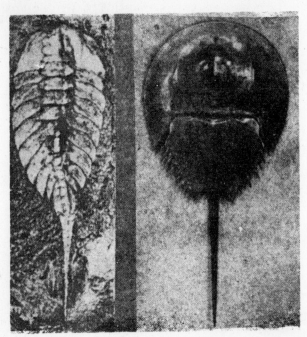

HORSESHOE CRABS

Figure 44. This fossil horseshoe crab, discovered by Charles D. Walcott of the U. S. Geological Survey, is over 500 million years old. Apparently it has taken a horseshoe crab over half a billion years to change from an oval to nearly a circular shape. He evidently belongs to a conservative family, but he has survived while the large family of trilobites perished. From *Origin and Evolution of Life* by H. F. Osborn of the American Museum of Natural History.

While some armored fishes were larger and could swim too fast to be killed by shellfish, yet they, too, at last became extinct. They were perhaps all killed by sharks.

Figure 47 is a picture of the armored fishes in the Devonian Period.

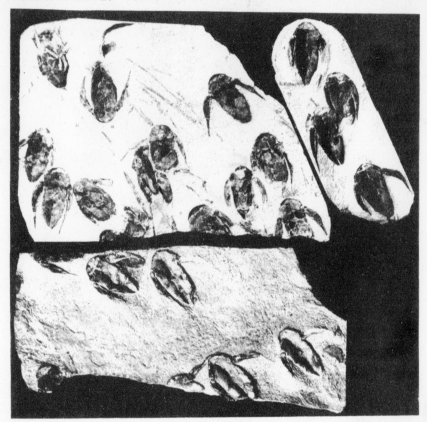

BOTHRIOLEPI

Figure 45. A group of Bothriolepi swimming up a stream in the Devonian Period in search of food near the place now called Miquasha, Province of Quebec, Canada. From *The Evolution of the Vertebrates and Their Kin* by William Patton of Dartmouth College.

You will recall that in the Silurian Period the plants were small, with very weak roots. Now in the Devonian

[102]

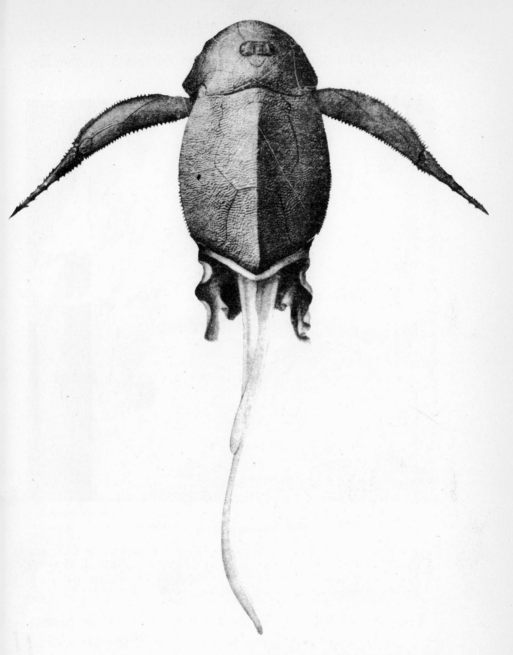

A FULL-LENGTH PORTRAIT OF ONE BOTHRIOLEPIS

Figure 46. He was about four inches long if we ignore his tail. Perhaps old Grandfather Thinopus ate him in those Devonian days as we eat lobsters now. From *The Evolution of Vertebrates and Their Kin* by William Patton of Dartmouth College.

ARMORED FISHES OF THE DEVONIAN PERIOD

Figure 47. These armored fishes show that it was not safe in those days for a fish to swim around without his coat of mail. Perhaps the fish nowadays refer to the Devonian Period as the "Mediaeval" or "Dark Age." Drawn by Miss Alice B. Woodward. From *Evolution in the Past* by H. R. Knipe, published by Herbert and Daniel, London.

Period the roots had grown stronger and the plants grew so large as to look like trees, sometimes forty feet high. They are called tree ferns. These tree ferns made the first great forests that spread over the earth. Compared with those of today they were queer-looking trees, as you can see from the pictures in Figures 48 and 49. A large forest of these tree-ferns grew at Gilboa, New York. Many fossil trunks, branches, and leaves have been found and are now in the New York State Museum at Albany.

You have probably seen a common weed called a horsetail. It is also known as a calamite and is one of the most ancient plants that we have. It appeared in the Devonian Period and then in the next period developed into a very large plant which looked like a tree, but it couldn't maintain so distinguished a position in the plant world. The big ones died, and now after millions of years only humble weeds have survived. We must always remember, however, that it had illustrious uncles in the ancient plant world.

Club mosses have the same family history as calamites. They are very common, and probably you have often seen them. They had begun to grow tall in the Devonian Period, and then after becoming as huge as trees the large ones perished and only the small ones survived. Ferns, too, are well-known plants which appeared in the world at this time.

The scorpions and centipedes which came from the water in the last period were now well accustomed to

A DEVONIAN FERN TREE

Figure 48. A 40-foot tree in the silent Devonian forest; for the scorpions and centipedes never spoke and Thinopus was not one of our noisy ancestors. After a drawing by Miss Winifred Goldring at the New York State Museum, Albany.

breathing air. A primitive winged insect probably flitted around among the trees of the Devonian forests for the first time in the history of the earth. Then there appeared a first spider.

You remember that the map of North America in the Silurian Period showed that the Gulf of Mexico extended in a long narrow sea north to the Gulf of St. Lawrence. Also you remember that such a sea is a weak place in the crust of the earth. In this period the place that yielded as the crust of the earth crumpled and folded was the part of the country now called New England, Nova Scotia, and New Brunswick. This folding made great mountains which covered the land and extended far out into what is now the sea, rising high in the air over the Newfoundland Banks, where today so many of our fish are caught (Figure 50).

South Carolina, North Carolina, and Virginia were also covered with mountains at this time. These folds and wrinkles caused the crust to crack so that masses of molten rock came to the surface. Sometimes this molten rock was very hard after it had cooled. In many cases the rock that we call granite is all that is left of the once majestic mountains that rose to the clouds. The White Mountains of New Hampshire are perhaps the granite cores of larger peaks that covered New England

Near the place that is now Montreal in Canada a small crack was made in the crust of the earth, and lava and hot gases were thrown out like water from a fountain.

A DEVONIAN FOREST WHICH COVERED A LARGE PART OF THE STATE OF NEW YORK

Figure 49. Perhaps old Thinopus wandered through this forest after leaving his footprints on the mud flats of Pennsylvania, for Gilboa, where these fossil trees were found, is not a great distance from Pennsylvania. After an exhibit made under the supervision of Miss Winifred Goldring in the New York State Museum at Albany.

The lava cooled after it had flowed a short distance, and so in the course of time it formed a mountain which, as

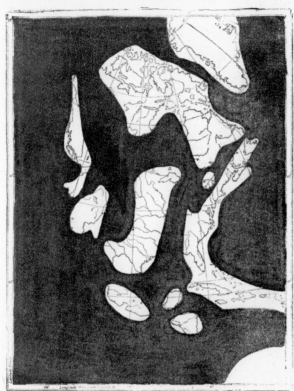

Courtesy of D. Van Nostrand Company

A MAP OF NORTH AMERICA IN THE DEVONIAN PERIOD

Figure 50. The outlines of this map have been derived from a drawing in *An Introduction to Historical Geology* by **W. J.** Miller. A modern outline map has been printed over the Devonian land areas to show the changes which have taken place (published by Rand McNally and Company, by whose permission the outline map has been reproduced).

you know, we call a volcano. This particular volcano is now named Mt. Royal. But it has been millions of years since Mt. Royal spouted lava from its crater, and now in winter it makes a wonderful toboggan slide.

Although along the Atlantic coast folds in the land caused mountains and volcanoes and made it very dangerous for animals, yet during most of the period a large part of the continent was very quiet. Shallow inland seas from time to time covered a large part of the country. In one of those seas a coral reef was formed at a place now occupied by Louisville, Kentucky. The Ohio River flows over this reef, which is so large that it causes rapids in that stream.

"Good bye, Fin!"

IX. CARBONIFEROUS PERIOD

WHEN we studied about the different kinds of gases in Chapter II, we learned that coal is made of atoms of C or carbon, and in Chapter V we learned how the chlorophyll in leaves kept the C it took from the CO_2. Our first great coal-beds were made in the period that we are now going to talk about. It has, therefore, been named the Carboniferous Period. It began about 300 million years ago and lasted 85 million years.

Coal-beds are made from peat bogs, and peat bogs are made from fallen trees, branches, and even leaves. To have peat bogs, however, it is necessary that there should be a great deal of low marshy country, you could never have a peat bog on top of a hill. Peat bogs are formed on low flat land near an ocean or lake. When the leaves, branches, and even the trunks of the trees fall into the swamp, they partly decay and crumble into small pieces and become what we call peat, and swamps of this kind are called peat bogs. When peat is dried it will burn slowly in a fireplace, and for this reason our great-grand-parents a hundred years ago or so used to dig peat and burn it as we now burn coal. In the Carboniferous Period the land was covered with dense forests of very tall tree-like growths which in the course of time fell and formed huge peat bogs which finally gave us the coal we find so useful.

Courtesy of Deutsches Museum, Munich, Germany

A FOREST IN THE CARBONIFEROUS PERIOD

Figure 51. From these swamps came peat bogs and then our coal-beds. Drawn by M. Potonie.

Figure 51 is a picture of a typical swamp forest in the Carboniferous Period. During this period there were vast swamps covered with these great forests. The air was warm and moist so that the trees grew rapidly. It was summer weather even in Greenland, and these huge trees grew there in those days; their fossil forms have been discovered by geologists. When a tree fell down, its place was quickly taken by new growth. The swamps, there-

Courtesy of the U. S. Geological Survey

DISMAL SWAMP, VIRGINIA

Figure 52. If not disturbed for a few million years this swamp might make first a peat bog and then a coal-bed. After a photograph by I. C. Russell, U. S. Geological Survey.

fore, soon became filled with partly decayed wood, and new trees grew on the rubbish of the old forests. Dismal Swamp (Figure 52) in Virginia is a living example of what these old Carboniferous swamp forests were like.

"THE MYSTERY OF THE FOREST"

Figure 53. Some of the tallest and oldest trees on the earth, the sequoias and redwoods, are found in the forests of California, Oregon, and Washington. After a photograph by H. C. Tibbits.

CARBONIFEROUS TREES

In this period the trees of the forests grew close together and had become tall, sometimes 100 feet or more high, but they were very different from the trees you are used to seeing. Besides the tall, tree-like ferns of Devonian time, there were now added to the forest some new and strange varieties which increased the weird effect of Carboniferous scenery.

Sigillariae (Figure 54) lived only in this period, but by their size and numbers they must have contributed greatly to our coal-beds. One fossil Sigillaria has been found which was six feet in diameter near the foot of the tree, and another one which measured 100 feet from end to end.

Very close cousins of the Sigillariae were the Lepidodendra (Figure 54), which also grew to be 100 feet high but had more slender trunks. Lepidodendra, unlike Sigillariae, developed many branches, but the leaves clung to the trunk and the main branches in the peculiar way that is shown in the drawing. This tree was a little more hardy than the Sigillaria, for it survived into the next period, when it perished.

The most important trees that appeared in this period were the Cordaites (Figure 54). They were the forerunners of the "big trees" of California, the giant sequoias and redwoods (Figure 53). Our own pine trees and spruce trees are also derived from this early family of Cordaites.

The small plants which we now call club mosses and

Figure 54. This swampy forest is forming a peat bog, which will eventually become a coal-bed. In the center background are Lepidodendra or giant club mosses. While the club mosses or running vines of today are not the direct descendants of these 100-foot treelike objects, yet they are descended from the same family. In the left background are Sigillariae and in the left foreground are Cordaites. Ferns and cycads are also in the left foreground. In the right foreground are "horsetails" or calamites. From a drawing by E. P. Blacknall in *Evolution in the Past*

horsetails were then huge trees or at least descended from the cousins of the Lepidodendra and calamites (Figure 54).

Then the earth's crust did some more wrinkling, and some of these great swamp forests sank a little so that water drained in and shallow inland seas formed where the trees had grown. In the course of time they became covered with mud and sand and sank farther down into the crust of the earth. It was hot down there—very hot; for the farther you go down into the earth, the hotter it gets. The peat formed by these fallen tree trunks was baked so thoroughly that there was almost nothing left but carbon. This was the carbon that had been taken from the air when the chlorophyll in the leaves of the trees absorbed the CO_2 from the air, kept the atoms of C, and let the atoms of O go free. Carbon from the old peat bogs that has been baked in this way we call coal.

Many times, after a peat bog had sunk, it was covered with mud enough to reach to the surface of the water. Then a new forest grew on this second swamp and there was formed another peat bog which in its turn sank and became coal. Of course when the peat was pressed and baked into coal the layers of mud were, at the same time and for the same reason, turned into rock. Sometimes the land rose again sufficiently to bring these beds of coal near the surface. Thus as we dig into the ground we occasionally find several beds of coal and between these beds layers of rock which had once been ancient mud.

When we put tons of coal into the cellar to burn in the furnace, it is interesting to think how long it took the Carboniferous forests to make the peat that was baked into this coal. It has been estimated that it took many centuries to make the peat for even a narrow seam of coal. Still more time was required to cover that peat bog with mud and to sink and bake it far down in the earth.

While they were alive, those vast forests were a wonderful home for new varieties of fauna. The Lepidodendra, the Cordaites, and their associates in the forests were the first trees to shelter the dragon-fly. In those days the dragon-fly was an imposing creature. To the smaller insects he must have seemed as large as an airship does to us. Some of these dragon-flies had bodies one and a half feet long and a spread of wings of twenty-nine inches (Figure 55). But at the same time and in the same forest there were tiny dragon-flies with wings only half an inch from tip to tip.

The ancient and well-known families of cockroaches, grasshoppers, and locusts appeared during this period. Of course they were all in a somewhat primitive state from our point of view. Yet, after all, they have changed surprisingly little in the last 200 million years.

Centipedes also flourished, for a fossil one was found at Mazon Creek, Illinois, that was twelve inches long and three-quarters of an inch thick. Some of its great compound eyes contained a thousand lenses.

Another emergence from the sea during the Carboniferous Period was that of the familiar land snail. It prob-

Courtesy of D. Appleton and Company

A DRAGON FLY'S ANCESTOR?

Figure 55. This fossil lived in the Carboniferous Period and is named Corydaleides. He was nearly a foot long. From *Geology* by Joseph Le Conte of the University of California.

ably isn't correct to imagine the first snail swimming through the surf, galloping up on the beach, and shouting to the first settler, "Scorpion! I am here." As with the other air-breathing fauna, its coming out of the sea and changing from the shellfish stage to the land-life stage must have been a long and dangerous experience. For millions of years many little shellfish probably learned how to shut themselves in their houses and keep from

THE UNCERTAINTY OF LIFE IN THE CARBONIFEROUS PERIOD

Figure 56. Bathing was dangerous in the warm waters of the Carboniferous Period. From a drawing by E. P. Blacknall in *Evolution of the Past* by H. R. Knipe, published by Herbert and Daniel.

drying up at low tide. Little by little and after thousands of fatalities, they learned to live a part of the time on land. Finally in the Carboniferous Period these snails joined the small circle of air-breathing fauna of which the descendants of old grandfather Thinopus were the leaders.

These descendants of Thinopus had grown so numerous that they had to earn a living in very different ways. Some found that they could get their food better by spending a large part of their time in the water. For such a purpose it was advantageous to have a long, slim body which could slip through the water easily; so, according to the well-known law of nature, some began to develop such shapes. Others stayed more and more on land and developed their legs for walking (Figure 56). Some of these amphibians were ten feet long and others were only six inches from head to tail. At Linton, Ohio, underneath a coal-bed, the fossils of over fifty different kinds of amphibia of this period have been found. Apparently they had at different times got stuck in a peat swamp, died there, and were finally buried by peat. Then when the peat was baked into coal they were baked into fossils.

Some fauna appeared during the millions of years of this Carboniferous Period which have always been very peaceful and unwarlike and which we, as well as the starfish, find very good to eat. They have been contented with sea life and have not tried to crawl up on the land. We call them oysters. Remember that the first primitive

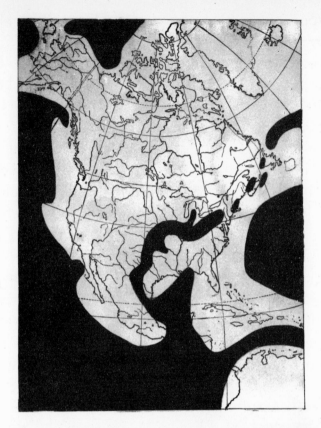

MAP OF NORTH AMERICA DURING THE LATTER PART OF THE
CARBONIFEROUS PERIOD

Figure 57. To show how much the geography of North America has changed,
an outline map by Rand McNally and Company has been printed over
the Carboniferous Period map. From a map in *Historical Geology* by
Charles Schuchert of Yale University, published by John Wiley and
Sons, Inc.

oyster appeared in this period along with the coal with which we now cook his descendants.

It is interesting to think how the map of North America looked during this period and how it had changed from the Devonian map as well as how it differed from the North America of today (Figure 57). You notice that what is now Greenland was then a part of the mainland of North America. If an amphibian of this age had wanted to, he could have crawled not only to Greenland but to Europe, for there was land all the way. Instead of finding great fields of ice he would have crawled through fine forests of such trees as calamites and Sagillariae. He would probably have had to dodge some of those foot-and-a-half dragon-flies and to have been careful not to disturb one of those Illinois centipedes. If he went by the coast he would have been wise not to swim too far into deep water, for there were many sharks in those seas.

The long, narrow sea which, in the last or Devonian Period, stretched from the water we now call the Gulf of Mexico to Newfoundland, you will notice has gone. Its place is now nearly all taken by dry land, and the only water is the irregularly shaped inland sea, consisting mostly of swamps, that extended across the Mississippi valley and south to Mexico. The black areas on the map are places that are now coal-beds which were formed during this period.

The disappearance of that long, narrow sea shows us

that the land at that place had begun to rise. The earth's crust had wrinkled again, and since this valley, filled with water, was the weakest place in this part of the world, the first wrinkle appeared here. The first effect of the slow folding of the crust was the raising of the bottom of this narrow sea. If fishes had been swimming in those days up and down this body of water, they would have found that the sea was becoming more shallow. Finally rocks would have appeared above the water. At last, those fishes of the inland sea would have lost their water and suffocated on the dry land which came in its place.

The crust of the earth moves so slowly that it is hard to imagine how long it took the bottom of this shallow sea to rise and make dry land. We think of the Egyptians as living in the very remote past—6,000 years ago; but it probably required 6 million years to turn this inland sea into dry land.

During the next period the crust kept on folding until a great mountain range miles high had risen where this Silurian sea had been. What is left of these magnificent folds we call the Appalachian Mountains. Thus the earth is ever changing, and sometimes very tiny movements that can hardly be noticed are the forerunners of mighty events in the history of geography; but before we can learn about that we will have to study in the next chapter about one of the most curious and interesting things in nature.

They call
me a
Tailpiece

X. GLACIERS

WE MUST first describe some very cold times that occasionally cover the earth with ice. It was during the period after the Carboniferous that one of these cold ages occurred, and since on at least seven other occasions a large part of the earth has been covered with ice, we will devote this entire chapter to a description of these strange happenings. We call such a cold time an Ice Age.

The world is so interesting and so full of strange things that when we start to tell a story about an Ice Age it is hard to decide just where we should begin. Let us commence with ice and try to find out what ice is and how it behaves.

We all know that when water is very cold it freezes and becomes ice. This happens at a temperature that we call thirty-two degrees. If you place a thermometer in ice-water and stir the water so that all the parts will be of the same temperature, the end of the little mercury column should be at exactly thirty-two degrees. This is one way of testing the accuracy of a thermometer, for if the end of the mercury column is one degree higher, that is, thirty-three degrees, or one degree lower, thirty-one degrees, then you will know that the thermometer is not just right.

Water is not the only thing that freezes. Almost everything freezes, and everything that does has a special temperature at which it becomes frozen or at which it melts. Most things around us are frozen or solid all the time; for example, candles, lead, iron, glass, and rock are usually in this frozen condition when we see them. If you have a very hot fire you can melt lead. Then you will find that it melts at 617 degrees. We can say that water freezes into ice at thirty-two degrees and that melted lead freezes into solid lead at 617 degrees. When liquid lava pours out of a volcano, it is very hot. The air is so much colder that the lava quickly freezes and becomes what we call rock, which is then just frozen lava. However, we are now more interested in frozen water and the way it behaves when a great deal of it is made.

When you look at snowflakes that have fallen on some dark cloth you will find that they are made of a great many very tiny crystals of ice. Before they melt you can sometimes see them through a magnifying-glass. Then you will find that these tiny crystals make very beautiful patterns (Figure 58). These crystals are just frozen particles of water.

You know how wet fog is. That is because it consists of little particles of water that are just as round as tiny balls. Each particle is so small that it is invisible to the naked eye. When the air is full of these little particles it is hard to see through it, and we then say it is a foggy day. Sometimes the fog is formed high up in the sky, and then we call it a cloud. When these little particles of water become crowded together in a cloud they will hit

SNOW CRYSTALS

Figure 58. Tiny snowflakes seen through a microscope. From *New Natural History* by J. A. Thomson.

each other and join together to form larger particles. Finally they get so large that the air cannot any longer hold them up in the sky and they fall down to the earth. Of course everything under that cloud gets wet and we say it is raining.

When it is very cold up in the sky—less than thirty-two degrees—then the little particles of water freeze into those tiny crystals which you saw on the dark cloth, and when they get crowded and come together they form snowflakes and fall to the ground. It is so cold on the tops of some high mountains that all clouds blowing over them become snowflakes and keep the tops of the mountains covered with snow and ice all the time. You may wonder where the ice comes from that is on top of a mountain when only snowflakes have fallen there. It is made from snowflakes, for when they are packed together in great piles and are very cold, they become one solid block of ice like the frozen water in our ponds in winter.

Ice behaves in a very curious way. If you hit it with a hammer it will crack and break like glass. On the other hand, if you leave the hammer on top of a block of ice, after a while it will begin to sink into the ice without a crack or a break. That is, if you press against ice hard and for a long time, it will bend just like putty; but if you hit it a sharp blow it will crack and break.

Ice is not alone in being so peculiar. Candles, glass, rock, and many other things behave in this way. You have probably seen a candle in warm weather keep bending very slowly until after several weeks it was pointing downward instead of up. Yet during all that time, if you had given that candle a sudden blow, it would have cracked and broken. A long glass tube will bend if you handle it gently, but as you well know, it will break if you strike it suddenly. Those great wrinkles in the earth

which formed the mountains were made so slowly that
the rock for miles would usually just bend without break-
ing or cracking. Of course sometimes the rock does crack
like a window pane, and then the land in the neighborhood trembles, and we call it an earthquake. But usually
the land bends so slowly that it takes millions of years to
form a wrinkle. Some parts of North America are bending now, but the movement is so slow that even the
change made in a hundred years would have to be measured by an expert.

Again let us return to the ice that has been formed
by countless millions of snowflakes high up in the mountains. This ice at first rests just where it was made on
the steep slope of the mountain. Like everything else on
a steep slope, if nothing prevented, it would slide down
to the bottom of the mountain. In this case it cannot slide
at once, for it is frozen into all the rough and uneven
places in the rock surface. However, that tendency to
slide to the bottom is always there; so the ice slowly
yields as it did to the hammer that started sinking into
the block. Little by little that great mass of ice moves
toward the bottom of the mountain. As the top of the ice
begins to move down like the candle, the bottom which is
frozen into the cracks and rough surfaces is forced to
come along also. If the mass of ice is very large—
perhaps hundreds of feet thick—the force of it is so great
that the bottom is carried right along with the top. The
great weight of the ice breaks away all the rough places

in the rock and carries all this débris down to the foot of the mountain. Such a great moving mass of ice sliding down the side of a mountain is called a glacier (Figure 59).

Glaciers move very slowly, for it takes ice a long time to bend into new shapes and flow down the sides of a

A GLACIER, LIKE A RIVER OF ICE
Figure 59. Chisana Glacier as seen from Eucher Mountain, Alaska.

mountain and then out over the land. Many travel only a few feet a day, although there is one in Greenland that moves sixty feet a day. When the glaciers reach the ocean as they sometimes do in Greenland, Alaska, and on the shores of the Antarctic continent, great blocks of ice break off and float out to sea (Figure 60). These floating pieces are called icebergs. They rise sometimes a couple of hundred feet from the surface of the water (Figure 61). They are very dangerous, for occasionally in a fog steamers run into them and sink.

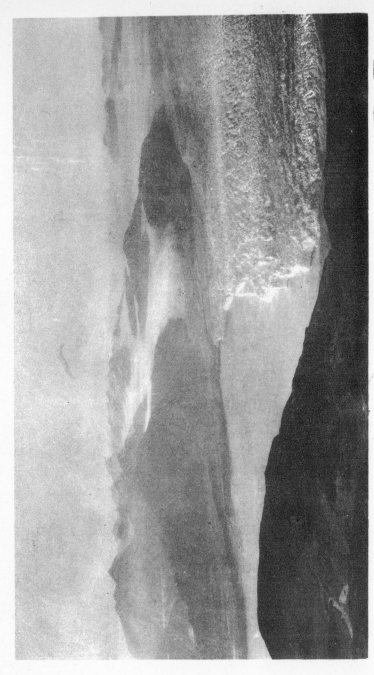

WHERE ICEBERGS ARE MADE

Figure 60. This is the great Muir Glacier of Alaska. It flows into the ocean, where large pieces break off and float away as icebergs. After a photograph by Harry Fielding Reid of Johns Hopkins University. The photograph was taken from an altitude of 3,000 feet on August 19, 1892.

ICEBERGS

The amazing thing about an iceberg is that there is
usually seven times more ice under water than you can
see above water. What we can see of an iceberg is so
large, it is hard to imagine how much bigger it really is.
If they were standing on the ground some would be as
large as a city block and as tall as a thirty-story building.
When such a giant mass breaks off from the glacier and
plunges into the ocean it makes a sound like thunder and
can be heard for miles around. Such huge waves rise
when the giant berg is launched into the sea that it is
dangerous for a vessel to go nearer than a mile. It almost
seems as if the iceberg were celebrating its joyous return
to the sea. For in the first place the sun had evaporated
the sea water and made those tiny balls of water which,
massed together, floated through the air as enormous
fleecy clouds. Then these clouds were blown high in the
air over the mountains and turned into crystals of ice
that formed snowflakes, which then fell on the mountain
and slowly formed that great glacier. Finally the glacier had moved down to the water and a big piece had
broken off and slid into the ocean. Sometimes it takes a
long time to melt one of these icebergs. They float from
Greenland far down into the Atlantic before the ice
melts and the tiny balls of water again join their mother
ocean.

A great quantity of water is always being held pris-
oner by these glaciers and ice-fields at the North Pole,
and the South Pole, and on the tops of the high moun-

Courtesy of the U. S. Coast Guard

ICEBERGS

Figure 61. "Only a small part of the 'berg' is above water, but this may be the longest, thinnest part of the mass, which projects like the apex of a floating cone." This iceberg was photographed from a U. S. Coast Guard cutter which

tains. It has been said that if all this ice were melted so that all the tiny balls of water could again be in the sea, the oceans would be so full that our beaches would be entirely under water. The water would even flow through the streets of many of our cities which are near the coast, such as San Francisco, New Orleans, Charleston, and New York. A large part of New Jersey, Florida, Louisiana, and Texas would be under water if such a thing happened.

It is interesting to remember that for millions of years in the Carboniferous Period there were no ice fields and no glaciers even at the North Pole. Instead of icebergs Greenland in those days produced wonderful forests which made peat bogs and coal-beds. Perhaps some day this will happen again. People will then live near the North Pole and have flower gardens, and those living in the cities on the coast will have to build their houses on higher land. Of course, if this state of things ever does come, it will come very slowly and take tens of thousands of years, which will give us plenty of time to prepare for it.

It is interesting in this connection to remember that during most of the history of the earth for the last 1,000 million years—that is, before our own history commences—Greenland was a warm and delightful place in which to live. Such a condition in Greenland seems to be the normal state, so that probably some day, perhaps 30,000 years from now, great cities will be built throughout Greenland where now the ice is perhaps a mile thick.

When great rocks or boulders from the sides of the mountain fall on glaciers they gradually sink through the ice to the bottom, and then they not only scratch the sides of the mountain but actually grind it into dust and wear it away; for the enormous weight of the ice, pressing on these boulders embedded in it, actually scrapes the rock as if it were clay. At the entrance to the American Museum of Natural History in New York City there is a large flat rock that has been not only scratched but quite deeply grooved by a glacier. The rocks that were carried down by the glacier were also often scratched. Like most glacial rocks the edges have been worn round because the rocks have been scraped and rolled over the bottom of the valley. The water that flows from the end of a glacier is so full of fine particles of rock that it looks gray. In the course of ages glaciers dig great valleys in the sides of mountains.

Sometimes in the past ages of the earth a glacier was so large that it flowed like a mass of cold molasses far out upon the land. Such a sheet of ice has been known to be a mile thick, so that it flowed right over all hills and even all but the highest mountains. We can now tell where it has been by finding scratches on the rocks of today (Figure 62). The direction in which these scratches point shows the path over which the glacier flowed.

THE MELTING OF A GLACIER

Where the glacier ended there are often great piles of rocks and gravel which were dropped by the ice as it finally melted (Figure 63).

If a season grew warmer after one of these ice ages, so that rain instead of snow fell on the glacier, rivers would

Courtesy of the U. S. Geological Survey

GLACIAL SCRATCHES

Figure 62. These scratches, running nearly horizontally over this smooth rock, were made by boulders embedded in the ice at the bottom of the glacier which once covered this ledge. These glacial scratches are near San Cristobal, Colorado.

be formed. After a short time these rivers would cut deep canyons in the ice and flow like a mountain torrent between great cliffs of ice or through tunnels in the ice. All the sand, pebbles, and even boulders that had been collected by the glacier would be carried by these streams out into the open country and spread on the land. We

[137]

find today all over the northern part of North America such mounds, and even hills of gravel and boulders, that were piled up by the last glacier that covered the land.

Glaciers change the shape of the valleys through which they flow. Nearly all valleys are first made by rivers. They are narrow at the bottom and wide at the top, much

Courtesy of the U. S. Geological Survey

ROCKS LEFT BY A GLACIER

Figure 63. This is a scene in Alaska where the Kotaina glacier melted and left these rocks and mounds of gravel.

like the letter V. After a glacier has ground and scoured the bottom of a valley for 100,000 years, it presents a very different appearance. The bottom becomes wide and the sides very steep. The U. S. Geological Survey illustrated this change, from a valley cut only by a river to one cut first by a river and then by a glacier, by drawings reproduced in Figure 64. Figure 19 is an example of a V-

A VALLEY CUT BY A RIVER

Courtesy of the U. S. Geological Survey

THE SAME VALLEY AFTER A GLACIER HAD PASSED THROUGH IT

Figure 64. Drawn by the U. S. Geological Survey. From *Introduction to Physical Geology* by W. J. Miller, published by D. Van Nostrand Company.

GOING-TO-THE-SUN MOUNTAIN

Figure 65. There was once upon a time a V-shaped valley in the Glacier National Park. Now it is U-shaped, due to the wear of the great glacial stream that flowed past the Going-to-the-Sun Mountain which is shown in the upper lefthand corner of the picture. After a photograph by T. J. Hileman.

shaped valley cut by the Yellowstone River. The valleys pictured in Figures 65 and 66 were once V-shaped valleys which have been scoured and rounded by glaciers.

We don't know why these great ice-fields came and covered whole countries with glaciers a mile thick. Also

Courtesy of Miss Beatrice M. Reed

YOSEMITE VALLEY, CALIFORNIA. EL CAPITAN ON THE LEFT AND CATHEDRAL ROCKS ON THE RIGHT

Figure 66. Before the glacier came, this valley was narrow with steep sides like the letter V. Then the glacier ground away the rocks and made the valley wide and round like the letter U. After a photograph by Miss Beatrice McCobb Reed.

we don't know why warm weather came again and melted the fields of ice. Perhaps it was because the earth wrinkled so much in some places and the land rose so high that it snowed during the whole year and then year after year. The ice that was formed in those places would never have a chance to melt and would grow deeper and deeper. Finally, it would spread in all directions until it covered whole countries. When perhaps after 100,000 years the land sank again or was worn down by the grinding of the ice, it would rain instead of snow and would melt the glacier by forming those great canyons through which the rivers rushed and carried boulders and sand with them.

Some think that an ice age is caused by a change in the amount of heat that the sun is giving us. They say that for some unknown reason the sun is sometimes a little brighter and sometimes a little fainter. Its being a little fainter for hundreds of thousands of years might cause an ice age.

Perhaps some day the cause of an ice age will be discovered and you will read about it in the newspapers and magazines.

"When's the next Glacier due?"

"Two million years and ten minutes, on track number four."

XI. PERMIAN PERIOD

NEARLY a hundred years ago an English scientist was asked by the Czar of Russia to study the rocks of the Ural Mountains. In this way the rock record of the period of earth-history next after the Carboniferous Period was discovered. Because it was in the province of Perm, in Russia, they called this the Permian Period. By "rock record" we don't mean that there were any words carved in the stone, but some things tell a story to scientists just as well as if whole pages had been written. For example, if you found the skeleton of Thinopus or any of his family you would know that the rocks in which the skeleton was buried must have been mud in the Devonian Period; for you remember that it was in that period that old grandfather Thinopus first made his footprint. This reading of the story of the earth from the rocks is very interesting.

The Permian Period began some 215 million years ago and lasted for perhaps 25 million years. This period was important for the descendants of Thinopus. They learned many tricks in those millions of years of which the old fellow never dreamed.

[143]

PERMIAN PERIOD

In the first place, one of those great ice ages occurred during this period. Perhaps it was the greatest ice age the earth has ever known. The ice covered most of South Africa, nearly all of India, and parts of Australia. Now you think of Brazil as a very warm country, but during the Permian Period there were ice sheets on its Atlantic coast even close to what is now the Amazon River. In North America there was a huge glacier where Boston now is and another over a part at least of the Gulf of St. Lawrence. The place now occupied by London was covered with ice.

The forests that grew in the nice warm air of that Carboniferous Period were suffering from winter weather that had not visited the earth before for millions of years. The great forest trees of Sagillariae, Lepidodendra, and calamites that helped to make the peat bogs which in turn became coal-beds, couldn't stand the snowstorms and died in large numbers. Some survived, but with stunted growth. At present, as you know, the survivors of this family are merely weeds—club mosses and horsetails. If you want to see trees stunted today by cold weather, all you need to do is to climb a mountain or travel far into northern Canada, Labrador, or Alaska. When you climb a mountain, the higher you get, the shorter you will find the trees; for it is increasingly cold as you climb higher and higher up the mountain. After a while you will get so high that it will be too cold and windy for even short trees, and you will find then only bushes and weeds. Then as you climb on, if the mountain is very high, you will leave all the bushes behind and come to only moss-covered rocks. Even moss can't live when it is too cold and windy; so you next find just plain rocks. Finally, on the very top you find that you are up in the sky among the clouds and that the ground all about you is covered with snow and ice. In the Permian Period the great fields of ice cooled the air so much that the trees grew smaller just as if the land had risen like a mountain.

Among the trees there was an energetic family that we have mentioned before, the family of Cordaites (Figure 54). Apparently the Cordaites were an independent family that didn't believe in doing exactly as their ancestors had done. Perhaps each tree differed a little from every other member of the family; some that happened to be tougher got along better than others which, like their ancestors, were soft and fond of warm air. So these trees kept on varying and changing, and those individuals that were best adapted to the increasingly cold seasons survived. Finally in this way a number of new kinds of trees appeared that have continued to grow even to the present time. The "big trees" of California (Figure 78) were developed at this time and are descended from this very independent and progressive family of Cordaites, as we learned when we read about the Carboniferous Period. You remember also that the spruce, firs, pine trees, and the great redwood trees of Oregon and Washington are cousins of the sequoia or "big trees," and all appeared at this time, taking the place of the fast-dying Carboniferous trees.

Trees were not the only forms of life that had to change their shape and size and methods of living on ac-

Courtesy Peabody Museum of Yale University

AN INSECT OF THE PERMIAN PERIOD

Figure 67. Dunbaria is the name of this beautifully preserved insect which lived in Kansas during the early part of the Permian Period. The color bands are plainly visible on the wings. It was found among the rocks of Insect Hill near Elmo, Kansas, by C. O. Dunbar of Yale University and was described and named by R. J. Tillyard, Chief Entomologist of the Commonwealth of Australia.

count of the cold winters. Those big dragon-flies of the Carboniferous Period couldn't stand the cold, and finally all perished in the Permian Period. The little dragon-flies and some other insects (Figure 67) were apparently tougher and so did not die out, for you have seen many of them flying about over ponds and streams. They are all descended from the tough little dragon-flies of the Carboniferous Period.

Down in Australia scientists have found a fossil beetle that lived during this period. He is the oldest beetle ever discovered. Like his descendants of today, he could survive the snowy winters and live in the neighborhood of great glaciers. His hard skin and ways of living were so well adapted to all kinds of weather that we have beetles now looking much like their old Permian ancestor.

The great glaciers on the shores of the continents must have filled the oceans with huge icebergs many times bigger than our present icebergs. Some of these glaciers were a mile thick. When they reached the ocean, blocks of ice a mile high fell into the sea. No ship today ever saw such icebergs. Some of these bergs with pointed peaks like mountains may have risen 1,000 feet above the waves of the sea. That would be twice as high as the Washington Monument. They would have extended many thousand feet under the water. It would have been a journey of miles to sail around one of those islands of ice.

No wonder the ocean grew cold as well as the land, so that the sea-dwellers had as hard a time as the calamites and Sagillaria trees. Some creatures, like the giant dragon-flies, had become too set in their ways and couldn't change. Those huge sea-scorpions that began their family history in the Silurian Period found the water too cold, and one by one they died and were eaten by their enemies. However, some humble cousins of these six-foot sea-scorpions were more lively and liked the cold water. They were a little different in shape, too, but still the family resemblance was very strong. These smaller fellows have survived to the present day and make a very popular food for all of us. We call some of them lobsters and some of them crabs.

In the world of fishes a very important change took place during this period. While the water was warm and food was plentiful a fish could earn a living even if he had a clumsy tail, for heretofore the backbone extended way down to one end of a fish's tail. You can see in Figure 68 what a clumsy-looking tail this made. In this period, however, the race for food and the running away from enemies made this funny tail a disadvantage. Those that happened to be born with a symmetrical tail could turn more quickly and dodge their enemies. So after millions of years most of the fishes which survived had the well-shaped tails that are the pride of our own fishes.

These hard times were caused not only by the cold winds from the glaciers and the oceans with many icebergs, but also by new wrinklings of the earth which made huge mountains rise. You remember that in the Silurian Period there was a long, narrow sea extending from the Gulf of Mexico to Newfoundland (Figure 32). Then in the Devonian Period the land rose so that this sea became shallow and there were mountains in the

Courtesy of J. M. Dent and Sons, Ltd.

FISHES WITH OLD-FASHIONED TAILS

Figure 68. These fishes with queer tails lived in the Silurian Period, perhaps more than 350 million years ago, and most fishes had queer tails until the Permian Period. From a drawing by T. Smit in *Nebula to Man* by H. R. Knipe.

place we now call New England. During this Permian Period this land continued to rise until there came those wrinkles in the crust which now we call the Appalachian Mountains. In those days when the mountains were young they were much higher than now. Some of the peaks were perhaps more than three miles high. The land at that time extended far out into the Atlantic Ocean, and nearly all of North America had risen so high that all inland seas except one had drained off. As you can see from the map (Figure 69), this sea covered that part of the country now called New Mexico, Arizona, Texas, Nevada, and California.

North of this sea was a land of many volcanoes. They are not there now, but in those days these volcanoes sent rivers of hot lava far out upon the land.

You will not be surprised then to learn that the amphibians—the family of Thinopus—were having a hard struggle to live. Figure 70 is a picture of some of these amphibians. Some were nine feet long and others only six inches long. Their favorite swamps of the Carboniferous Period had become dry land, so that they had to live on the banks of rivers or on the edge of that sea that covered the State of Utah. Some amphibians were therefore crowded out of the water and forced to hunt for their food on land far from the sea. That was a difficult thing for them to do, for like old Thinopus they had always crawled on the land and dragged their stomachs on the ground. In the search for food in the forest those that

Courtesy of D. Van Nostrand Company

MAP OF NORTH AMERICA IN THE PERMIAN PERIOD

Figure 69. In order to show the difference between a Permian map and a modern one, an outline map of recent date has been printed over the outlines of the ancient continent. The Permian map is based upon a drawing in *An Introduction to Historical Geology* by **W. J.** Miller. The outline map was made by Rand McNally and Company, by whose permission it is here reproduced.

could travel only in this slow way went hungry. Probably many of this distinguished family died from starvation, because they had been crowded out of the rivers, and in

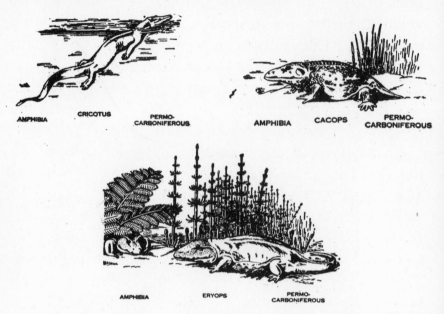

Courtesy of Charles Scribner's Sons

AMERICAN AMPHIBIA OF THE PERMIAN PERIOD

Figure 70. At the beginning of the Permian Period the Amphibia had developed into a variety of forms. Cricotus was probably known among his associates as a famous swimmer. Cacops was too stout for his length. Eryops was noted for having a head which was almost solid. The best we can say for them all is that they were just a little brighter than fishes. After a drawing by W. K. Gregory and Richard Deckert at the American Museum of Natural History. From *Origin and Evolution of Life* by H. F. Osborn.

dark forests they were too slow to catch bugs. Fortunately for us, some neither starved nor stayed on the river banks. These were the amphibians that happened to have stronger feet, so that they could move faster. This was a great advantage and in the course of millions of years a race of strong-footed creatures was developed; for in each generation the best runner got the most food, while many of the slow ones starved. Finally these creatures learned to live on land and to breathe air exclusively and never went near the water. We call them reptiles (Figure 71). For about 160 million years the reptiles were the most powerful animals in the world.

Although the change from the amphibian to the reptile was very gradual and took millions of years, yet we think of one animal as the founder of the group, because his fossil skeleton is that of the oldest reptile that has been found. His name is Varanops. Since he represents one of our remote ancestors and the founder of a new era in our family history, we should hang his portrait in our dining-room beside that of Thinopus. Figure 72 is a full-length portrait of Varanops.

Like all families, the descendants of Varanops moved into many countries and began to live in varied ways. This finally made them look different from each other, and each had his own pet form of behavior (Figure 73). Some began to have heads like dogs (Figure 74). You notice their teeth are more like those of a dog or cat than like those of a reptile, and teeth are a very important part of any reptile. These reptiles are called "beast-shaped." They were the most intelligent animals that so far had come upon the earth, and it was this branch of the reptile

PERMIAN REPTILES

Figure 71. A scene in the Permian Period. Perhaps these reptiles, which were
until recently amphibians, are starting to explore the land, where they
were destined to rule for four geological periods, or about 160 million
years. Drawn by Miss Alice B. Woodward for *Evolution in the Past*
by H. R. Knipe, published by Herbert and Daniel.

family which in a very indirect fashion was perhaps closely related to our ancestors.

The amount of brains that an animal has is fairly well indicated by the way in which he gets his food. In all ages the animals that kill and eat other animals or that can escape quickly are usually brighter and quicker than

Courtesy of the University of Chicago Press

VARANOPS

Figure 72. A reptile which lived in Texas during the Permian Period. He was about 4 feet long. From *Water Reptiles of the Past and Present* by S. W. Williston of the University of Chicago.

the ones content to eat only leaves and grass and to move slowly. It required more brains to catch an amphibian and conquer him than to eat plants; so the bright ones enjoyed a meat diet. In the course of time the brightest, quickest, and bravest of the meat-eaters learned how to catch a variety of animals. Such were the beast-shaped reptiles of which the dog-tooth Scymnognathus was a good example. If a reptile eats nothing but bugs and just

[155]

A SCENE IN THE EARLY PART OF THE PERMIAN PERIOD

Figure 73. The amphibian Eryops is crawling out of the water and is being chased by a cotylosaur. This is a family quarrel, for the cotylosaur is a cousin of Eryops. The cotylosaurs were a very energetic branch of

sits by a log to catch insects that come near, he becomes lazy and stupid; but if he roams in the forest and either overtakes his prey or sometimes lies in wait for it, he has to do a little thinking as well as a little running. Just as the reptiles were brighter and stronger than the amphibians, so after millions of years the beast-shaped reptiles were the brightest and strongest of all the reptiles.

Courtesy of Charles Scribner's Sons

SCYMNOGNATHUS

Figure 74. A dog-toothed reptile related to the ancestors of the mammals. After a drawing by W. K. Gregory and Richard Deckert at the American Museum of Natural History. From *Origin and Evolution of Life* by H. F. Osborn.

Before the end of the period some of these beast-shaped reptiles had developed most unusual forms (Figures 75 and 76). They were called "fin-backed" reptiles and were savage creatures that killed and ate not only amphibians and smaller reptiles, but perhaps each other. We do not know what use they had for those high fins on their backs. Perhaps the fins were for the sake of appearance and made the owners more attractive to each other. Men, you know, sometimes wear very high black silk hats called "stove-pipes" because they think it makes them more attractive. Therefore we must not be too harsh in criticizing the artistic taste of these Permian reptiles.

Courtesy of the University of Chicago Press

DIMETRODON IN TEXAS

Figure 75. About 200 million years ago Dimetrodon with bright eyes and smiling mouth was proud of his magnificent fin back. He belonged to the ruling class in Texas. From *Water Reptiles of the Past and Present* by S. W. Williston of the University of Chicago.

We ought not to leave the Permian Period without mentioning the salt-beds of Kansas and Germany. The movement of the land drained, and the dryness of the air evaporated many lakes and inland seas. The gradual drying of a large inland sea or lake made smaller salt lakes. You remember how Lake Bonneville gradually dried up and grew smaller until it formed our present Great Salt Lake in Utah. In Kansas, in the course of thousands of years salt-beds 200 feet thick were formed

Courtesy of the American Museum of Natural History

DIMETRODON IN NEW YORK

Figure 76. What a change 200 million years can make! Dimetrodon, 8 feet long and 4 feet high, is now an exhibit at the American Museum of Natural History, New York City.

and buried far down beneath the surface of the earth. When wells are bored into the ground these salt-beds are found over an area of about 100,000 square miles. It is estimated that they contain thousands of millions of tons

[159]

of salt—the greatest mass of salt that has ever been discovered in the earth. The next greatest salt-beds are in
Germany. In some places these beds are 3,000 feet thick.

Some beds of salt have been mined for hundreds of
years. There is a famous salt mine in Austria where handsome rooms have been carved in the rock salt.

The King of the Permian Age

XII. TRIASSIC PERIOD

THE next three periods are sometimes called the Age of Reptiles. The descendants of our friend and ancestor Varanops became very numerous and powerful. For over 100 million years they ruled the air, land, and sea. They learned to fly and swim. Some that stayed on the land became the biggest, heaviest fauna that have ever lived on the earth. You remember that these reptiles came into existence at the time of great disturbances. There were earthquakes; glaciers a mile thick were spreading over the land; huge icebergs were floating in the ocean, and the land was rising and drying up the swamps when Varanops learned to be a reptile and to live without going in bathing. Like human beings, his descendants became very set in their ways, and after 100 million years or more they became a bit old-fashioned. Then another of the earth's revolutions came and utterly destroyed them. It is odd that, having been born as it were in one revolution, they couldn't stand another. When you study history you will find that many of our families today resemble their magnificent but unfortunate reptilian ancestors.

TRIASSIC PERIOD

The next period, and the first of the Age of Reptiles, is called the Triassic. It began perhaps 190 million years ago and lasted about 35 million years. All the ice of the Permian Period had disappeared, and during most of this time the air was warm and dry even near the North Pole,

Courtesy of the Princeton University Press

TRIASSIC FERN

Figure 77. A giant broad-leaved Triassic fern which grew in Virginia and North Carolina. From *Plants of the Past* by F. H. Knowlton of U. S. Geological Survey.

and there were dense forests in northern Greenland. In Virginia and North Carolina there were giant ferns (Figure 77), and the tall sequoias and redwood trees grew all over our continent as they do now in California, Oregon, and Washington (Figure 78).

Some of these great trees fell into an inland sea and

[162]

THE BIG TREES OF CALIFORNIA

Figure 78. These sequoia trees are a part of Mariposa Grove (Yosemite National Park), the last of a mighty race of giants which millions of years ago covered a large part of North America. (*The Big Tree and Its Story*, by G. H. Sherwood, American Museum of Natural History.)

floated south to Arizona, where they were buried in the mud. After millions of years in the ground they were turned to stone. Then the overlying rocks were gradually worn away. and now in Arizona we can see the stone

Courtesy of the U. S. National Museum

PETRIFIED TREES

Figure 79. Three petrified logs of the Triassic Period in the Fossil Forest Park, Arizona. After a photograph in the U. S. National Museum.

trunks of these trees lying on the ground. Some are eight feet in diameter and 120 feet long. The government has set aside this land as a national park (Figure 79).

Although the reptiles ruled most of the land, they were not at peace. They quarreled, and even ate each other.

Perhaps that was because they became so numerous that they had to fight to get enough to eat, and this struggle for food became so fierce that some reptiles went back to the shore and got their food by killing some of the members of that old family founded by our great-grandfather Thinopus which had remained amphibians and had not

Courtesy of Charles Scribner's Sons

PLACOCHELYS

Figure 80. After a drawing in *Origin and Evolution of Life* by H. F. Osborn of the American Museum of Natural History.

changed into reptiles. Then these reptiles became bolder and actually went into the water after fishes just as their ancestors had done. After millions of years they changed their shapes for the same reason that we have described many times before. Some developed hard shells to protect themselves against their enemies. Figure 80 is a picture of one of these old reptiles that returned to a seafaring life. You can readily see that he was the ancestor of our turtles, sometimes called chelonians. Those feet with five toes now had to turn back to the shape of a fin or paddle.

It had taken the fish a long time to change his fin into a five-toed foot (Figure 39). Now, in order to get more food, that foot had to change again to something as near a fin as possible. By comparing Figure 39 and Figure 81

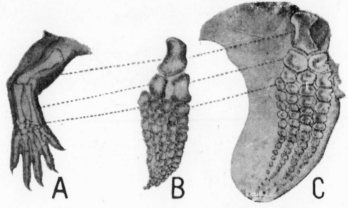

THE CHANGE OF A FOOT TO A FIN

Figure 81. A picture to illustrate the change of a foot during millions of years into a fin or paddle. From *Origin and Evolution of Life* by H. F. Osborn of the American Museum of Natural History.

you will see that the foot never did change completely into the kind of fin that the original fish had had, but still it served its purpose very well and sent this old chelonian through the water with considerable speed.

Members of another branch of the reptile family which were obliged to return to the water in order to get food are called plesiosaurs. Old Lariosaurus was the founder of this branch of the family, and his full-length portrait is given in Figure 82. A few million years later, these plesiosaurs found it advisable to change their shape a trifle, as you can see from the picture (Figure 83). At the

Courtesy of Charles Scribner's Sons.

LARIOSAURUS

Figure 82. A reptile which returned to the water and lived on fish. He was the ancestor of the plesiosaurs. Drawn by Deckert after McGregor, at the American Museum of Natural History. From *Origin and Evolution of Life* by H. F. Osborn.

end of the Age of Reptiles they perished. Perhaps they were eaten by sharks, or perhaps they couldn't stand the cold period. Therefore, they are not our ancestors. They are merely some poor relatives who failed in the struggle for existence.

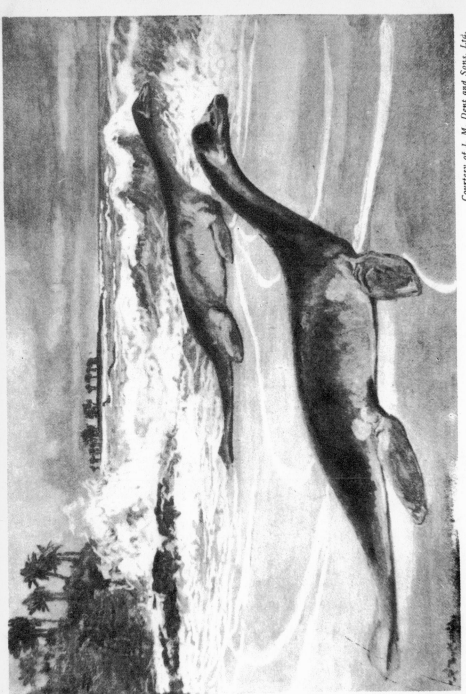

PLESIOSAURS

Courtesy of J. M. Dent and Sons, Ltd.

Figure 83. Sometimes a plesiosaur sat on the beach and watched the wild Cretaceous waves roll in. Drawn by E. P.

ICHTHYOSAURS

During the fierce fights for food some reptiles were pushed farther and farther into the sea until finally only those survived that could live in the water all the time. Therefore their shapes were very much changed, as you can see from the picture of one of them (Figure 84). They are called ichthyosaurs, which means fish-lizards. Later they roamed the sea and killed many large fish. We

Courtesy of Charles Scribner's Sons

CYMBOSPONDYLUS

Figure 84. A Triassic ichthyosaur. He had a very interesting family tree of ancestors. Far back in the Silurian Period his ancestors were fishes. In the Devonian Period they partly left the water and became amphibians. In the early part of the Permian Period they left the water entirely and became reptiles. They returned to the banks of the streams and behaved like amphibians. Finally in the Triassic Period Cymbospondylus stayed in the water all the time and behaved like his remote ancestors the fishes. After a drawing by W. K. Gregory and Richard Deckert of the American Museum of Natural History. From *Origin and Evolution of Life* by H. F. Osborn.

will meet them again before we finish with this Age of Reptiles.

The most interesting reptiles were those that learned to walk on their hind legs. They and certain of their relatives who walked on all four legs are called dinosaurs. Perhaps we can regard Anchisaurus as the founder of this family. Anchisaurus (Figure 85) was a savage creature. He believed in fighting and never ate anything but raw

[169]

ANCHISAURUS

Figure 85. Anchisaurus is here shown in this Triassic forest. He is looking across the pool at those old-fashioned amphibians. After a drawing by E. P. Bucknall for *Evolution in the Past* by H. R. Knipe, published by Herbert

meat. In a fascinating book called *Evolution of the Past*, by H. R. Knipe, an English scientist, it is recorded that Plato, a famous Greek, who lived about 2,000 years ago, once tried to describe man in such a way as to show how he differed from all other animals. He finally concluded that the two things that made a man different from all other forms of life were that he had no feathers and that he walked on two feet. Of course Plato had never heard of Anchisaurus, who exactly fits this description.

Some of the descendants of either Anchisaurus or his contemporaries learned how to eat plants and leaves. The more leaves they ate, the more they lost their taste for meat. When we change from eating beefsteak to eating beans no important change takes place in our shape, but with dinosaurs it was very different. After millions of years the dinosaurs that liked meat for their meals became very different from their cousins who liked leaves and plants. When a dinosaur who ate flora felt hungry he walked up to a bush and began eating. He could walk as slowly as he pleased, for the bush wouldn't run away from him; also, the bush wouldn't fight to defend itself. So the dinosaur that lived in this way gradually lost the ability to run fast and to conquer his prey. He became very lazy, and since there were plenty of green plants and leaves to eat he grew large and had heavy, thick feet. Figure 86 is a picture of one of these vegetable-eaters, named Plateosaurus, whose ancestors not very far back had given up their meat diet. Before the Age of Reptiles was over these plant-eaters grew to an immense size. Some weighed 80,000 pounds and were tall enough to have eaten from the roof of a two-story house. In a later chapter we will learn more about them and how they perished at the close of the Age of Reptiles.

Courtesy of Charles Scribner's Sons

AN ANCESTOR OF LEAF-EATING DINOSAURS

Figure 86. This is a picture of Plateosaurus. He was one of those peaceful dinosaurs that killed and ate only bushes and plants. His hind legs have already begun to grow thick and heavy. His descendants have legs like elephants. From *Origin and Evolution of Life* by H. F. Osborn of the American Museum of Natural History.

No great range of mountains rose during the Triassic Period. However, the land was far from being quiet and peaceful. All along the Pacific coast of North America from California to Alaska volcanoes spouted flames and ashes high in the air and rivers of hot lava flowed down their sides. An inland sea covered the part of the country

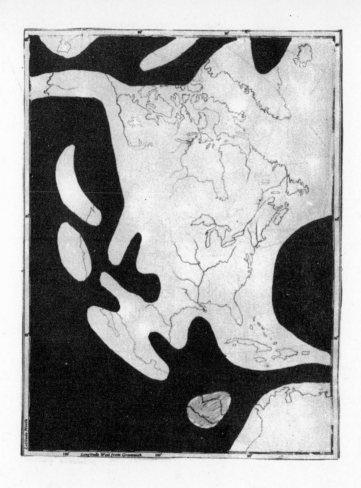

MAP OF NORTH AMERICA DURING THE LATTER PART OF THE
TRIASSIC PERIOD

Figure 87. In order to compare the Triassic map with the present one an out-
line map of North America at the present time by Rand McNally and
Company has been faintly drawn over the land areas. From a map in
Historical Geology by Charles Schuchert, published by John Wiley and
Sons, Inc.

Courtesy U. S. Forest Service

BASALTIC COLUMNS

Figure 88. Devil's Post Pile, National Monument on San Joaquin River, Sierra National Forest, California. Many tourists are sitting among the fallen columns. After a photograph by the U. S. Forest Service.

now called California, Oregon, Washington, and British Columbia, and from this water rose countless volcanoes. The lava from these volcanoes can still be found on the land in those places. The map (Figure 87) shows not only the inland sea but the land to the west, which extended far out into the Pacific Ocean. Now, of course, that land is no longer there; for millions of years ago it disappeared into the depths of the ocean. Over Arizona you can see in the map the inland sea through which perhaps those great trees floated before they were buried and became fossilized.

The north Atlantic coast was also disturbed. Cracks that extended for many miles appeared in the earth. In some places the land on one side of a crack would rise hundreds of feet in the air and the land on the other side would sink equally far, so that great cliffs were formed. From these cracks there sometimes flowed masses of melted rock or lava. When this lava cooled it often formed long six-sided columns packed close together. They are called basaltic columns. The Palisades on the west bank of the Hudson River were made of basaltic rocks that came out of the earth at this period. At the same time Mount Tom in Massachusetts, the East Rock at New Haven, and Orange Mountain in New Jersey were formed. This series of cliffs, with here and there fairly well-made six-sided columns, extends across Pennsylvania and Maryland to Virginia. The picture of the Devil's Post Pile (Figure 88) is an excellent example of these basaltic columns, which in some cases instead of being six-sided are five- and even seven-sided.

In the Triassic Period the land extended far out into the Atlantic Ocean on the east coast of North America, as you can readily see by looking at the map, and the land near these cliffs of basaltic columns was dry like a desert.

If you go through this part of the country you will find a great deal of red sandstone that was made at this time. For some of the rock contained iron ore, and when particles were worn away and became mud in the valleys, the iron ore made the rock red. Then in time the mud was pressed into rock and became the well-known red sandstone which is so typical of this part of the country. Sometimes you will find foot-prints of dinosaurs in this red sandstone. A number of these footprints have been cut from the rock in the Connecticut River valley and taken to the Peabody Museum of Yale University at New Haven (Figure 89).

The forests during the Triassic Period must have been a wonderful sight. As we said, there were tall sequoia and redwood trees and quantities of cycads (Figure 90) that were much like those living today. Few, if any, colored flowers had appeared as yet. You would have missed the birds also, if you had been there; for nothing flew in the air except a few large insects and some dragon-flies and a strange flying dragon which you will learn about in the next chapter.

ANTS

If you had looked at the ground under those giant trees and near the cycads, you probably would have found some of those remarkable little creatures that we call ants. They were the first of the fauna to help each other and to divide their work with their neighbors. This was a great event in the history of the earth. Hundreds of

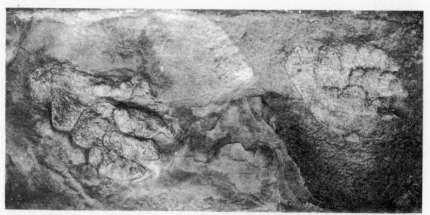

Courtesy of the Peabody Museum of Yale University

"FOOTPRINTS ON THE SANDS OF TIME"

Figure 89. One of the largest dinosaurs walked over a mud flat and left an immortal footprint for Yale. After a photograph of an exhibit at the Peabody Museum of Yale University.

millions of years earlier the little individual cells had united into groups and divided the work of living among them. As you probably remember, some cells protected the group with a tough outer layer and others caught the food. It was probably in the Triassic Peroid that the second step in coöperation was taken, when a little group of ants began helping each other instead of fighting each other. Although the earliest fossil ant so far discovered lived a few periods later (Oligocene), yet it is probable that the ants began their career in this period.

CYCADS

Figure 90. Living cycads in Japan. After Wieland. From *Plants of the Past* by F. H. Knowlton of Princeton University.

Perhaps in the future the nations of the earth will be wise enough to cause a third great event in coöperation to happen, when they will try to help instead of fighting each other. There isn't room in this book to describe the way in which ants live, but they probably lived in the

DROMATHERIUM

Triassic Period about as they do today. You will read some day how they build houses for each other and hold little aphids as servants, just as we do cows and horses. For some unknown reason the ants never grew large. If they had grown to be as large as horses they might have controlled the earth. Their wonderful capacity and their instinct to help each other would have made them the rulers of the earth. They probably would have killed all animals that were their enemies, just as we are doing today. Under such conditions the cousins of the apes would never have had an opportunity to become men. Yet a book much like this would probably have been written by the older ants to tell the younger ones how the world was made. Possibly the ants by this time would have had schools and colleges and large buildings. Fortunately for us, the ants never grew larger and never changed their way of living.

While you were looking on the ground at those very intelligent ants in the Triassic forests, you might have heard a rustling under some cycads, and then perhaps you would have seen a very small animal about the size of a squirrel climb up one of those redwood trees for safety. You would have seen one of your ancestors—the first mammal. Dromatherium (Figure 91-A) is his name, and the picture of his jawbone should hang in your dining-room; for he was the founder of your group of mammal ancestors.

As we have said before, a founder of a new line of ancestors like Dromatherium didn't suddenly appear in a new form so different from that of his reptilian parents. Dromatherium was almost exactly like his parents, and his parents were almost like his grandparents. The change from the reptile had been very gradual. Millions

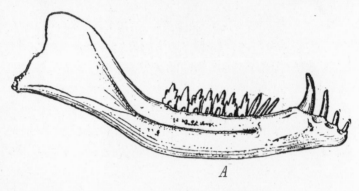

A

DROMATHERIUM

Figure 91. All that we can find of Dromatherium, who was the first distinguished Virginian. However, Dromatherium probably very closely resembled Ptilodus, who is here pictured as he probably appeared in the Cretaceous Period. The drawing of Dromatherium is after H. F. Osborn, courtesy of the American Museum of Natural History. The picture of Ptilodus is a restoration from *History of Land Mammals in the Western Hemisphere* by W. B. Scott, published by The Macmillan Company.

of years were required to produce this new form. Dromatherium, the founder of this new type, was found in Virginia, and we have found none of the skeletons of his immediate ancestors. He was descended from some cousins of the beast-shaped reptiles that are described in Chapter XI. A picture of this cousin is given in Figure 74.

Dromatherium and his friends were insignificant compared with their enemies, the dinosaurs. However, the mammals had one great advantage that was destined to make them the ruling animals. The mothers nursed their children, who were therefore guarded, fed and trained

B

PTILODUS

Figure 91.

while they were young. Reptiles laid eggs and then usually went off and left them. The poor little reptiles had to struggle out of the shells as best they could. Immediately they had to hunt for their food and if possible avoid their enemies. Many perished, and few of them received any training from their parents, so that what the parents learned in their lifetime was not handed down to the children. But the mammals in that far-off Triassic Period began to teach and to train their children. At the present time some of the mammals not only train their children at home but send them to school and to college, for people are mammals. Cats, dogs, lions, tigers, horses, cows, and our cousins the apes and monkeys, are also mammals.

Thus at the end of the Triassic Period we find there had been evolved mammals—the highest type of animal so far produced on the earth. They were the natural result of incessant warfare—of killing and eating. Countless millions of individuals had been sacrificed in this struggle. During all this period of perhaps 800 million years almost every individual met with a tragic death. A few, perhaps, died of old age or of disease; but most jellyfish, fishes, dragon-flies, amphibians, and reptiles were killed and eaten by their enemies, and this fierce condition exists today, not only among the fishes, insects, amphibians, and reptiles, but also among the mammals; for tigers, lions, gorillas, and men still fight both for food and for a place in which to live.

"They didn't have books in my day"

XIII. JURASSIC PERIOD

THE next period was determined by the famous English geologist, William Smith, who lived during the early part of the last century. However, the period was named Jurassic by a French geologist, Alexandre Brogniart, because he found in the rocks of the Jura Mountains between France and Switzerland a more complete record of it than had been previously discovered. This period began about 155 million years ago and like the Triassic Period lasted for about 35 million years.

In the preceding period a very important piece of progress took place, for some of the small reptiles learned how to fly. You remember that back in the Carboniferous Period, about 100 million years earlier, from jointed sea-worms crawling up on the land in search of food had developed the flying creatures known as dragon-flies. Then in the Triassic a reptile, perhaps because he too was hungry, learned to travel through the air and swoop down in flight upon his food. Now in the Jurassic Period flying became more common, for two kinds of reptiles had taken to the air.

Two very queer things happened to some of these reptiles. In the first place their scales turned into feathers, and then the feathers made the wings. It isn't understood just how feathers came to be worn by birds, for we have never found any fossil remains of a bird that had a skin which was partly scales and partly feathers. Perhaps some day you may find such a fossil, and then you can learn just how scales were able to change to feathers. Birds with these primitive half-formed feathers probably lived in the previous or Triassic Period. After you have learned how to read the record in the rocks, you may explore some Triassic rocks and find this early bird.

The most ancient bird that has ever been discovered was found in the Jurassic rocks of Germany. His name is Archaeopteryx. He was mostly covered with fine feathers (Figure 92), but his head had few feathers and showed his reptilian ancestry. He had a scared look, and well he might, for he was a feeble flier, like all beginners, and there were fierce dinosaurs waiting for an opportunity to eat him.

Although we don't know just how feathers were developed, we think we know how birds learned to fly. Apparently some little reptiles were forced to live in the trees on account of the danger of being eaten by the big dinosaurs. These little reptiles jumped from the trees on any tiny animals wandering under the branches of the tree that looked good to eat. If some had long, flat scales that projected out from their limbs when they jumped, they would glide down to the ground a little

ARCHAEOPTERYX

Figure 92. Bird life in the Jurassic Period. Archaeopteryx is clinging to the
tree by the claws on his wings as well as by the claws on his feet. He was
probably a meat-eater and ate small animals and insects more often than
fruit. After a drawing in *The Origin of Birds*, by Gerhard Heilmann,
published by H. F. and G. Witherby, London.

more easily. If their scales were light instead of heavy, that would make the fall to the ground easier. This might give them an advantage over the others so that after a while there would grow up a race of small reptiles with feathers which would project from the sides of all four legs and make the landing on the ground not quite such a blow (Figure 93). Then the feathers grew thicker and longer, always because those with thicker and longer feathers could jump farther for their food and so had a better chance to live and raise a family of very primitive birds. Finally, the feathers were so many and so long that the little reptile could guide himself somewhat by flapping his forelegs. Then gradually the forelegs grew longer and were covered with longer feathers, and the hind legs grew shorter and were covered with shorter feathers. This continued until at last they were able to fly back to the branch of the tree from which they had jumped. Now we call them birds. Mr. Beebe has made a drawing (Figure 94) to show how a bird's wings were developed.

Archaeopteryx, who met with an untimely death by falling into the mud, and who thereby preserved his skeleton and feathers for our inspection, still retained some very reptilian habits. He ate little animals as his ancestors had done when they used to jump from the branches of the trees. He still kept his teeth, as you can see by examining his picture, and his head was more scaly than it was feathery. Also, he kept his claws on his front legs or wings, as they are now called, so that he could

LEARNING TO FLY

Figure 93. The first attempts at flying by a primitive bird. After a drawing
in *The Origin of Birds* by Gerhard Heilmann, published by H. F. and
G. Witherby, London.

cling to the branches of trees as you can see in his picture. Archaeopteryx didn't sing like a song sparrow; his voice was probably harsh and made a sound more like croaking than like singing. You may wonder how we can know anything about his voice; for certainly a fossil doesn't speak, and a voice cannot be caught in the mud and

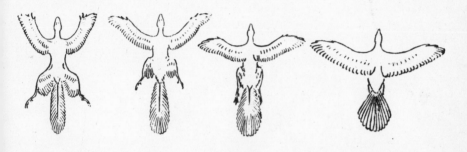

Courtesy of Charles Scribner's Sons

HOW ARMS TURNED INTO WINGS

Figure 94. Four stages in the development of a bird. After Beebe. From *Origin and Evolution of Life* by H. F. Osborn of the American Museum of Natural History.

turned into stone. You remember that all through the ages we have found that some children were not just like their parents, and that their parents were not just like their grandparents. In this way in the course of time new kinds of animals were developed. At the same time some of their cousins would not change. These cousins would be like their parents and their grandparents. You will recall that this was true of the little bacteria way back in the dim past. Then there were the horseshoe crabs as an-

HOATZIN

Figure 95. A young hoatzin climbing. He is using those claws on his wings which he inherited from his remote Jurassic ancestors. After a drawing in Hutchinson's *Animals of All Countries*.

other example. Now Mr. Beebe has described a bird living in South America today which is very much like
Archaeopteryx. This bird has lost his teeth and has more
feathers on his head than Archaeopteryx; yet apparently
he hasn't changed much from his old ancestor. His name
is hoatzin (Figure 95), and his voice is more like that
of a reptile than that of a bird.

In a very entertaining book, *Animals of the Past*, by
F. A. Lucas, we read: "Mr. Quelch, who has studied
these curious birds in their native wilds of British Gui-
ana, tells us that soon after hatching, the nestlings begin
to crawl about by means of their legs and wings, the well-
developed claws [on their wings] being constantly in use
for hooking to surrounding objects. If they are drawn
from the nest by means of their legs, they hold on firmly
to the twigs, both with their bill and wings; and if the
nest be upset they hold on to all objects with which they
come in contact by bill, feet, and wings, making considerable use of the bill with the help of the clawed wings,
to raise themselves to a higher level."

In the next period the descendants of Archaeopteryx
lost their teeth and the claws on their wings, and became
more like modern birds.

The reptiles found that there was more than one way
of making a wing, and they proved it by forming two sets
of flying creatures at the same time. These rivals of the
birds were also their cousins and are called pterodactyls
or "flying dragons" (Figure 96). In the next period,

PTERODACTYLS

Figure 96. These pterodactyls have just left their home on some cliffs in
Kansas and are starting on one of their fishing trips over the shallow
Kansas sea. From a drawing by Miss Alice B. Woodward in *Evolution
in the Past* by H. R. Knipe, published by Herbert and Daniel, London.

called the Cretaceous, the pterodactyls grew so large that they were twenty feet from tip to tip of their outspread wings. They were the largest creatures that ever learned how to fly and were more like bats than like birds, for they had neither scales nor feathers. Their wings were enormous sheets of skin, and in order to be light the bones were hollow and filled with air. But while they looked like bats they were neither bats nor the ancestors of bats, for bats are mammals and are descended from the little primitive mammals like Dromatherium of Virginia, which at this time was running for his life from dinosaurs, from birds with teeth, and from these same "flying dragons."

The pterodactyls probably learned to fly as the birds did, but instead of developing their scales into feathers, they abolished their scales altogether and developed a loose skin that gradually spread between their forelegs and their hind legs. This is not so unusual, for you know how in a duck's foot the skin has gradually spread between the toes so that we call ducks "web-footed." Ducks are birds which, because they were hungry, began a long time ago to hunt for food on the banks of streams and ponds. Little by little they learned to swim to get their food and to escape from their enemies. Those that happened to have broad feet could swim faster, could get more food, and had a better chance to raise a family of little ducks. These little ducks inherited their parents' broad feet, and so in time they grew to be web-footed.

Courtesy of Charles Scribner's Sons

FLYING SQUIRREL

Figure 97. "At times one would be seen darting from the topmost branches of a tall oak and with wide extended membranes and outspread tail gliding diagonally through the air, till it reached the foot of a tree fifty yards off, when, at the moment we expected to see it strike the earth, it suddenly turned upwards and alighted in the body of the tree. It would then run to the top and once more precipitate itself from the upper branches and sail back again to the tree it had just left. Crowds of these little creatures joined in these sportive gambols; there could not have been less than 200." From *The New Natural History* by J. A. Thompson, published by G. P. Putnam's Sons. The drawing is from *American Natural History* by William T. Hornaday, published by Charles Scribner's Sons.

FLYING SQUIRRELS

Then there are the flying squirrels that instead of feathers or wings have developed a loose skin that spreads between their feet when they jump from a tree (Figure 97). In this way they soar instead of really flying, just as Archaeopteryx did when he first began to

Courtesy of the "Aeronautical Journal"

THE BEGINNING OF A FLIGHT

Figure 98. Illustration of the soaring flight of a pterodactyl. After a drawing in the *Aeronautical Journal*, London. From *Age of Mammals* by H. F. Osborn of the American Museum of Natural History.

jump from a tree and use his feathers. If human beings don't exterminate the flying squirrels, in a few million years they may be able to develop like pterodactyls and soar for hundreds of miles over the forests.

Perhaps the pterodactyl always started his flight by jumping from a cliff (Figure 98), just as his ancestors had done when they used to jump from a tree. Then he probably soared like a hawk. In this he was very skillful, for there is reason to believe that in the next period he used to start from the chalk cliffs of Kansas and soar for hundreds of miles over the shallow sea that covered a part of the great western plains in those days of the remote Cretaceous Period.

The greatest of all pterodactyls is called Pteranodon (Figure 99). This is the creature whose spread of wings measured twenty feet. He was carefully studied by S. P. Langley, Secretary of the Smithsonian Institution at Washington, when he was devising one of the first flying-machines; for Pteranodon was one of the most perfect flying devices that the fauna of the earth had ever created.

In *Flying Reptiles*, W. D. Matthew says that Pteranodon was "a marvelously elaborate mechanism, gigantic in size, perfected in every detail of adaptation to its singular mode of life, automatic and precise in its response to every gust of the changing wind, to every distant flicker of light or shade that might indicate some prospect of prey or warn of lurking enemy. I can see him soaring as the great sea birds do today, sweeping tirelessly across the broad glittering surface of the Cretaceous seas, patrolling them from dawn to dark in search of such unwary fish . . . as might be sunning themselves at the surface and come within reach of the sudden swoop from above. . . . At night he would perhaps return to the

THE GREAT PTERODACTYL PTERANODON

Figure 99. He glided for hundreds of miles over the Kansas seas. Drawn under the direction of S. P. Langley of the Smithsonian Institution at Washington.

shore many, many miles distant and hang himself upon some favored roost—tree or rocky point—anywhere that would be securely out of reach of the dinosaurs and other fierce reptilian beasts of prey which lived upon the land."

The condor and the albatross are our largest flying birds, and it is therefore interesting to compare the skeleton of a condor with that of Pteranodon (Figure 100). The dotted lines show the space occupied by the wings.

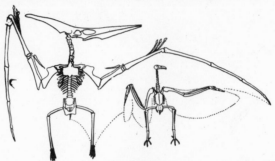

Courtesy of the American Museum of Natural History

PTERANODON AND THE CONDOR

Figure 100. The great pterodactyl Pteranodon compared with the condor, one of the largest of living birds. From *Animals of the Past* by F. A. Lucas of the American Museum of Natural History.

Just how a pterodactyl walked is a puzzling problem. Some had no tails, and the picture (Figure 101) may indicate how they folded their wings and walked away. Some, however, had long tails like Dimorphodon (Figure 102). Perhaps the tail helped to balance so large a head. When Dimorphodon was in a hurry he looked something like an old-fashioned cavalry officer with spurs and long saber and a fierce expression.

TAILLESS PTERODACTYL

One of the best fossil pterodactyls (Figure 103) can be seen at the Peabody Museum of Yale University, and

Courtesy of D. Appleton and Company

CYCNORHAMPHUS

Figure 101. A small tailless pterodactyl. Drawn by Miss E. B. Seeley for *Dragons of the Air* by H. G. Seeley of the University of London.

another fossil skeleton is on exhibit at the American Museum of Natural History of New York City.

The Jurassic must have been an interesting period for the dinosaurs and primitive mammals (Figure 104). From time to time as they met in the forest (Figure 105) they probably discussed the latest flying exploit. Perhaps some favored the pterodactyls and others the birds. Then

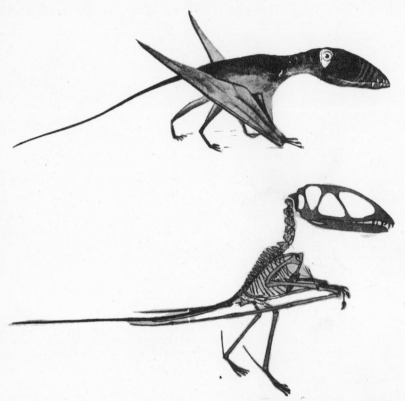

Courtesy of D. Appleton and Company

DIMORPHODON

Figure 102. *Upper.* A little long-tailed pterodactyl. *Lower.* As he may have walked when in a hurry. Drawn by Miss E. B. Seeley for *Dragons of the Air* by H. G. Seeley of the University of London.

there may have been rivalry between the long-tail and short-tail "dragons of the air," to see who could soar the farthest over the shallow inland seas (Figure 106). What rejoicing there must have been on the plains when Pteranodon first made a non-stop flight across the Mississippi Valley! Unlike Lindbergh, he probably had to flee from

Courtesy of the Peabody Museum of Yale University

A FALLEN PTERODACTYL

Figure 103. A fossil long-tailed pterodactyl. After a photograph of a specimen in the Peabody Museum of Yale University. "One of the very few examples showing the imprint of the wing membrane."

the reception committee of dinosaurs or he would have been eaten alive.

It was a flying time—this middle period in the Age of Reptiles. Maybe encouraged by the example of the reptiles, some insects began to fly. For millions of years, ever since the Carboniferous Period, the dragon-flies had ruled the air. Now they were no longer safe when flying; for

[201]

Courtesy of J. M. Dent and Sons, Ltd.

"A GOOD TIME WAS HAD BY ALL"

Figure 104. In the Jurassic Period you naturally fought to get your food and then you fought to keep it. We must always remember that in many cases food for one is death for another. To the one who does the killing and eating the world is bountiful; to the one who is killed and eaten the world is barbarous. After a drawing by C. Whymper for *Nebula to Man* by H. R. Knipe.

A JURASSIC FOREST

Figure 105. Perhaps they are all exchanging news as they meet in this luxuriant forest. Drawn by E. P. Bucknall for *Evolution in the Past* by H. R. Knipe, published by Herbert and Daniel, London.

Figure 106. Pterodactyls are sometimes called flying lizards. Some of these natives of Kansas had tails and some had not. After a drawing by Miss Alice B. Woodward for *Evolution in the Past* by H. R. Knipe, published by Herbert and Daniel, London. *Courtesy of Miss Alice B. Woodward*

FOSSIL MOSQUITOES

Pteranodon and Archaeopteryx must have enjoyed swallowing nice fat dragon-flies. The dragon-flies' humiliation must have been complete when another little insect

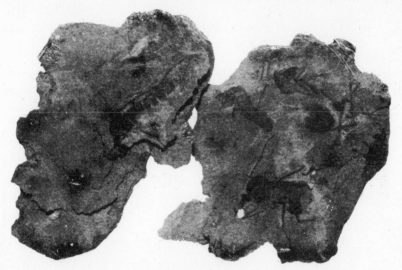

Courtesy of the American Museum of Natural History

FOSSIL MOSQUITOES

Figure 107. When giant dinosaurs roamed over the land, these huge mosquitoes also flourished. They are not the direct ancestors of our own dear mosquitoes, but they are their cousins, who lived in what is now called the Gobi Desert in Asia. These fossils were found by the expedition of the American Museum of Natural History, and the photograph was published in *Natural History*.

began to fly. His name is mosquito (Figure 107), and he has been a nuisance ever since he developed wings.

Bees, flies, and butterflies appeared in this flying period. Gradually the forest was beginning to be filled with insect life, including bright-colored butterflies. In the next period we will see how the flowers spread over the land and, with the birds and insects, made the world look modern.

During the Jurassic Period the air was warm, and deep forests grew in Greenland, for then that name would have been appropriate. During most of the time the land was quiet so that the dinosaurs.were not shaken by earthquakes and were not frightened by rivers of lava from bursting volcanoes. However, toward the close of the period great changes took place on the Pacific coast of North America. As in the Triassic Period, numbers of volcanoes, from California to Alaska, spouted lava. In addition, the hot interior of the earth seemed to get restless and boiled up through the crust, pushing the rocks and their fossils high into the air; some of these blocks of rock were hundreds of miles long, and when one edge was very much more elevated than the other, some of our grandest mountains were formed. Such were the beginnings of the Sierra Nevada Mountains, the Coast Range, and the Cascade Mountains. Between the Sierra Nevada Mountains and the Coast Range a valley was formed, and we now call this land the Great Valley of California (Figure 108).

At the same time the land where the Rocky Mountains now stand sank. You have already found that such a long, narrow depression in the crust of the earth usually precedes the formation of a great chain of mountains. You remember that before the Appalachian Mountains rose at the end of the Permian Period there was for mil-

Courtesy of D. Van Nostrand Company

A MAP OF NORTH AMERICA IN THE JURASSIC PERIOD

Figure 108. A modern outline map has been printed over this Jurassic map in order to show the contrast between the modern and ancient geography. (Outline Map, published by Rand McNally and Company, by whose permission it is reproduced.) The Jurassic map has been modified from a drawing in *Introduction to Historical Geology* by J. W. Miller, published by D. Van Nostrand Company.

Courtesy of J. M. Dent and Sons, Ltd.

CERATOSAURUS

Figure 109. This dinosaur lived in Colorado in the Jurassic Period. Since he was a meat-eater and about 20 feet tall, it is not surprising that the small mammal in the lower righthand corner of the picture should hide under the ferns. That small mammal looks as if he might have been a close relative of our direct ancestors of that period. He resembles that distinguished Virginian, Dromatherium, whom we met in the Triassic Period. Until the dinosaurs became extinct the mammals found it was safer to live in the trees or hide under the bushes. After a drawing by T. Smit from *Nebula to Man* by **H. R. Knipe.**

lions of years a long, narrow sea extending from the Gulf of Mexico to the Gulf of St. Lawrence (Figure 32). Also you will remember that this long, narrow sea became a weak point in the earth's crust so that when the earth cooled a little more and grew a little smaller the crust wrinkled, where there had been the long, narrow sea, and made the Appalachian Mountains. In the next period we will find that this same thing is happening again, only this time on the Pacific coast. We will see before long the great Rocky Mountains rising where the map in this Jurassic Period shows a long, narrow valley (Figure 108).

The hot melted rock came up so quickly when the Coast Range and Sierra Nevada Mountains rose that many small cracks were formed in the land as it was pushed up. Some of these cracks were filled with a melted white rock called quartz. You have probably seen quartz crystals in museums. This white-hot melted quartz carried with it a very valuable and rare metal—gold. During the millions of years that followed, the surfaces of these mountains crumbled into rocks and dust; for you remember that the atoms of O in the air are always attaching themselves to the rocks and making them crumble. Then rain came and washed all the pieces down into the valley. This quartz containing the small particles of gold crumbled with the rest of the rock and was washed down the sides of the mountains by streams and rain. In this way some of the quartz became ground into very fine dust and the little particles of gold were set free. In 1849 a man found that some of the soil in this Great Valley of California was full of these little free particles of gold. Since then many millions of dollars' worth of gold have been taken from the California ground. Some of this very hot melted rock that was forced through the cracks of the earth at this time contained copper and silver as well as gold.

The poor little descendants of Dromatherium of Virginia continued to have a hard time, for the mammals were still so small and timid that "none could look a

"I wish that Big Boy would hurry up and become extinct!"

dinosaur in the face," according to Professor Schuchert of Yale. Figure 109 shows how carefully the descendants of Dromatherium had to hide from the dinosaurs. Dinosaur Ceratosaurus is the villain's name in this picture.

These queer dinosaurs with horns are found only in North America, but the American Museum of Natural History found their ancestors in Asia. All these horned American dinosaurs are called Ceratopsia. They must have walked all the way from what is now the Gobi Desert in Asia by way of Siberia and Alaska and settled in Colorado and Wyoming where the food was plentiful; and in those days there were no Indians to shoot them. In the next period these great dinosaurs became extinct and the little mammals in their turn grew large and began to rule the world.

XIV. CRETACEOUS PERIOD

WE HAVE now come to the last and a very long period in the Age of Reptiles, the Cretaceous Period. It began about 120 million years ago and lasted for perhaps 65 million years.

During most of this time the air was warm. In Greenland and Alaska there were forests of cinnamon trees, fig trees, tree ferns, laurel, and many other plants that are now found only far south of the Arctic Ocean. It was so warm that there was no cold weather even in Greenland. During half the year the nights there were long and dark just as they are today; but the air was so warm and moist that the trees grew through all the year. No man was there to watch them grow, and the armored dinosaurs and flying dragons made no records of it. However, the trees themselves made a record; and we can read that record in the fossil tree trunks which we find in Greenland and Alaska.

When you cut down a tree or saw its trunk in two, you will find a large number of rings marked in the wood. They will start with a very small ring in the center and end with a large ring just inside of the bark (Figure

110). If the tree was just eight years old when it was cut down, you will be able to count eight rings; for a new ring is grown each year. When you find the stump of a

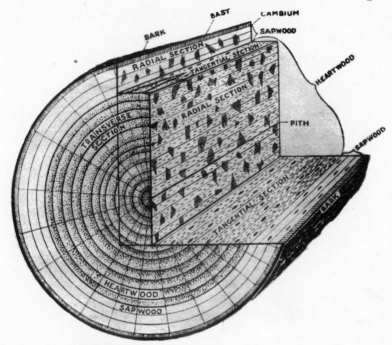

Courtesy of Ernest Benn, Ltd.

ANNUAL RING GROWTH OF TREES

Figure 110. A diagram to illustrate the annual ring growth of trees. From *A Text Book of Wood* by Herbert Stone.

large tree you can always tell how old it is by counting the number of rings. These rings are made because the tree grows only in summer. Each winter the tree stops growing or grows only a very little, and each summer it adds a new layer of wood around the old growth. If it were summer all the time and the air were moist and warm all through the year, the tree would grow a little every day. Then the rings would be very indistinct and you would have to have bright eyes to see them. If the tree became a fossil these faint rings would disappear. So when we find fossils of large trees in Greenland and Alaska and cannot find any rings of growth, we know that they grew all through the year and that the air was moist and warm in winter as well as in summer. Some day you may study rings of growth in the great redwood and sequoia trees of the Pacific coast. Then you will be able to tell the years in the history of North America that were rainy, when the trees grew rapidly, and those that were dry, when the trees grew slowly; for when the tree has plenty of water to drink, it grows well and adds that year a thick ring of wood, but when there is a dry year and the tree is thirsty most of the time, it grows very slowly and adds only a very thin ring of wood to its trunk.

While the trees were flourishing it was a very bad period for mountains. During those long millions of years the mountains were crumbling and the pieces were being washed down into the valleys until only low hills were left and the ocean spread over the land, forming large, shallow inland seas. On the edges of these seas great swamps and peat bogs were formed which later became submerged and were baked into the coal that is found all the way from Canada to Arizona. In Colorado alone it is estimated that there are 34,000 million tons of the coal of the Cretaceous Period.

Another thing that we use much as we do coal was made during this period. It is oil, called petroleum, from which gasoline and kerosene are made. When a little shell fish dies tiny globules of oil that were in its body escape to the water, for all fishes, you know, are very oily. If the water is clear these small globules of oil rise to the surface, where they are lost and gradually disappear. On the other hand, if the water is muddy and not too much disturbed by swift currents, these tiny globules attach themselves to the little particles of mud; for the globules of oil and the particles of mud are very friendly and always get together if they can. After a while the mud settles to the bottom of the shallow sea and carries its little oil companions with it. Then the mud is sometimes buried deep in the earth and is compressed into rock. We dig wells in this rock and pump out the oil. In Wyoming and Texas, and especially in Mexico, we get much oil from rock made out of the mud of the Cretaceous Period. From one well in Mexico 40 million barrels of oil were taken in five years.

During most of this period of low, well-rounded hills and many shallow seas and swamps, the Mississippi River did not flow into the Gulf of Mexico but across the Great Plains into the Pacific Ocean. It probably flowed through Arkansas. It was a long journey in those days for the little drop of water that joined the Ohio

River near where Pittsburgh is now and slowly flowed down the rivers and across the broad Mississippi valley and the plains of Arkansas, Texas, New Mexico, and Arizona. Finally it joined the great Pacific Ocean. During this journey that drop of water would have seen some of the most remarkable animals that ever lived on the earth.

You remember that way back in the Triassic Period the reptiles had broken up into groups which became so different from each other that some lived on the banks of shallow seas and ate leaves and plants, and some lived in the forests and ate the animals that they could catch.

These meat-eaters became in this Cretaceous Period the most powerful and ferocious land animals that have ever lived. They came from a long line of many generations in the Triassic Period in which Anchisaurus, walking on his hind legs (Figure 85), was a famous member. During the Jurassic and Cretaceous Periods his descendants became bigger, swifter, and more cruel, until they ruled all the forests and plains and shores. We call such a giant king of the tyrant lizards *Tyrannosaurus rex*. In the American Museum of Natural History you can see a magnificent skeleton of this king lizard (Figure 111). *Tyrannosaurus rex* was so tall that he could have seized a pterodactyl from the top of an ordinary telephone pole. The old tyrant didn't eat vegetables with his meat, but he did eat those cousins of his whose only food was vegetables.

[216]

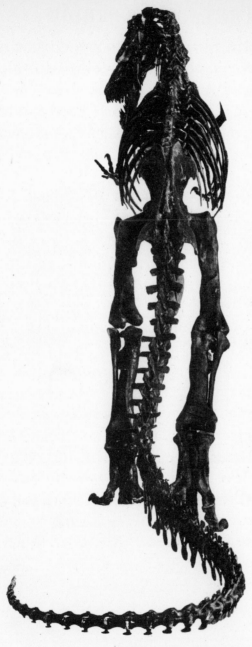

TYRANNOSAURUS REX

Figure 111. A destroyer of the leaf-eating dinosaurs. A photograph of a skeleton in the American Museum of Natural History.

CRETACEOUS PERIOD

These peaceful cousins were obliged to grow some very strong armored skin to protect themselves against the meat-eaters. Of course you will at once say that this dinosaur armorplate came into existence from purely natural causes, because only those with hard skin ever survived. After millions of years some survivors became like little

"TRICERATOPS, HE OF THE THREE-HORNED FACE"

Figure 112. Members of the dinosaur family of Ceratopsia, which were often attacked by the savage *Tyrannosaurus rex*. After a model by C. R. Knight at the American Museum of Natural History.

walking forts. Some are called Triceratops (Figure 112), because they had three horns on their heads, and *tri* means three. You remember old Ceratosaurus, who made little Dromatherium hide under the cycads in the Jurassic Period (Figure 109). He also belonged to this group of Ceratopsia.

Another dinosaur found it was safer, when *Tyrannosaurus rex* was around, to carry his protection with him. His name is Stegosaurus (Figures 113 and 114). Being

[218]

very large and well protected, he didn't have to think much. At least we suppose he didn't, for the bony part of his head which held his brain was extremely small.

One family of peaceful, leaf-eating dinosaurs protected themselves by growing to an enormous size. They were the largest animals that ever walked on land. One was Diplodocus and another was Brontosaurus (Figure 115). Imagine Brontosaurus in a field today, 16 feet high, 70 feet long and weighing 70,000 pounds. He weighed as much as five African elephants. It must have been hard work for his mouth to eat enough leaves to keep his stomach from being always hungry, for it is believed he had to eat 700 pounds of leaves a day to keep from starving. These leaf-eaters had ancestors in the Triassic Period. Plateosaurus (Figure 86), whom you have met before when you traveled through the Triassic Period, was a prominent leaf-eater in that earlier time. Even in those ancient days Plateosaurus had been eating his meals from the neighboring bushes for so many generations that he had developed rather large and clumsy feet. You remember he didn't have to run to catch a bush, for the bush always stood very still and let him walk up slowly and eat it. Therefore he didn't need spry little feet for running and jumping, but he did need large, round feet so that he could stand for hours and eat the leaves from a tree or wade in marshy places without being mired. You notice that in the Cretaceous Period the descendants of Plateosaurus had feet like those of ele-

STEGOSAURUS IN WYOMING

Figure 113. From a painting by C. R. Knight in the Field Museum of Natural History, Chicago.

STEGOSAURUS AT YALE

Figure 114. In the Cretaceous Period this dinosaur lived at Medicine Bow, Wyoming. After the last geological period he moved to the Peabody Museum at Yale University, where he now resides.

BRONTOSAURUS

Figure 115. This giant leaf-eating dinosaur lived in the shallow seas in Wyoming and Colorado where the Rocky Mountains now stand. After a painting by C. R. Knight made under the direction of H. F. Osborn

phants; that is, Brontosaurus and Diplodocus had feet that were very good to stand on but not so good for running. Sauropods is the name given to these giant leaf-eating dinosaurs with elephant feet.

The sauropods had good reason not to be friendly with their cousins the meat-eaters; the American Museum of Natural History has found the skeletons of two dinosaurs which had been overwhelmed by some accident while one was eating the other (Figure 116). The meat-eater in this picture is a cousin of *Tyrannosaurus rex*, and his "dinner," an unfortunate sauropod, was a cousin of Brontosaurus.

On another occasion we can only guess who won, for in Figure 117 Tyrannosaurus is about to attack Triceratops, who always carried his fort with him.

In the Triassic Period you will remember that a family of reptiles made their living by catching fish in the sea. Their family name is Ichthyosaur. The portrait of the founder of the family is given in Figure 84, and his name is Cymbospondylus. The name sounds as if he were a foreigner, but he was not; he belonged to one of the old reptile families who had become fishermen. In the Cretaceous Period this family became very numerous and very powerful. In Figure 118, a mother ichthyosaur, perhaps twenty-five feet long, is seen followed by her family.

Those who bathed in the seas of Kansas in the Cretaceous times must have been ever dreading the mosasaurs.

THE END OF A FIGHT BETWEEN GIANTS

Figure 116. (Above) The sad death of a leaf-eater that met a meat-eater one Cretaceous day. A cousin of *Tyrannosaurus rex* has defeated a member of the family of the giant Brontosaurus. After a painting by C. R. Knight made under the direction of H. F. Osborn. (Below) A photograph of mounted specimens at the American Museum of Natural History, New York City.

A FIGHT BETWEEN GIANTS

Figure 117. The "tyrant" dinosaur *Tyrannosaurus rex* about to attack the horned dinosaur named Triceratops. After a painting by C. R. Knight under the direction of Henry Fairfield Osborn from mounted specimens at the American Museum of Natural History, New York, N. Y.

ICHTHYOSAURUS

Figure 118. A Jurassic fish-lizard. Mother with a brood of young. After a painting by C. R. Knight under the direction of H. F. Osborn for the American Museum of Natural History.

Courtesy of the University of Chicago Press

GEOSAURUS

Figure 119. A mosasaur that lived in the Jurassic Period, a cousin of Tylosaurus but not so large. After a drawing in *Water Reptiles of the Past and Present* by S. W. Williston, Professor of Palaeontology in the University of Chicago.

CRETACEOUS PERIOD

In the Jurassic Period, when the mosasaurs had even then become well adapted to life in the water, they had an amusing expression (Figure 119). In the Cretaceous Period, however, they had become, perhaps, the **rulers of**

TYLOSAURUS

Figure 120. A giant mosasaur from the inland Cretaceous seas of Kansas chasing the fish named Portheus. After a drawing by C. R. Knight at the American Museum of Natural History.

the seas, just as *Tyrannosaurus rex* had become the ruler of the land. The head of the family in Cretaceous times was named Tylosaurus. His headquarters were in the shallow seas that covered a large part of Kansas. There he caught large fish (Figure 120), and his descendants became so numerous that bones of a thousand mosasaurs have been taken from the chalk cliffs of Kansas. This ruler of the Cretaceous seas was sometimes forty-five feet long and more dangerous than are the man-eating crocodiles of India.

The ichthyosaurs and mosasaurs had rivals, the plesiosaurs. We read about plesiosaurs in the Triassic Period (Figures 82 and 83), and now in the Jurassic and Cretaceous Periods we find them fighting for their share of the food in all the shallow seas. The plesiosaur has been described by F. A. Lucas as "a snake threaded through the body of a turtle." This was how he looked, but of course he had no shell. During this, the last period in the life of plesiosaurs, some grew to be forty-five feet long.

In the Triassic Period we found that some reptiles, in order to avoid their enemies and get enough to eat, had adopted the seafaring life so completely that they had become chelonians or turtles. Placochelys (Figure 80) was a distinguished ancestor of this family. The chelonians, however, believed in progress, followed the fashions of the Cretaceous Period, and grew large. The giant sea turtle Archelon (Figure 121) illustrates how well the chelonians imitated the other giants of the Cretaceous Period.

Even one of the birds grew large in this giant period. His name is Hesperornis (Figure 122). Apparently for millions of years some of the descendants of Archaeopteryx of Germany (Figure 92) had been in the habit of

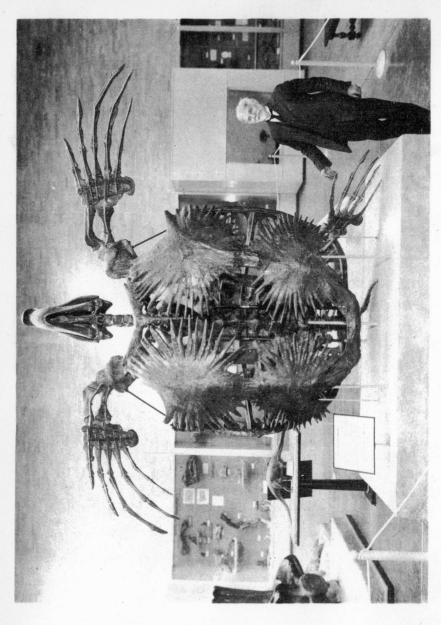

THE GIANT SEA TURTLE ARCHELON

Figure 121. After a photograph of a specimen in the Peabody Museum of Yale University.

catching small fishes that swam in the shallow pools. Little by little these birds learned to dive into deeper water and to swim back to the shore. Those that couldn't do this probably starved, while those that could dive and swim not only had plenty to eat but also brought up

THE GREAT TOOTHED DIVER HESPERORNIS

Figure 122. Covered with smooth soft feathers, this bird caught fishes by diving, but he lost the art of flying. After a drawing by J. M. Gleeson at the American Museum of Natural History.

families of little birds to be good divers. After a long time these birds gave up flying altogether and caught all their food by diving for fish. There must have been plenty of fish, for the birds grew so large they couldn't have flown if they had wanted to. Then their wings became a nuisance, for the wings must have made it hard for them to dive through the water rapidly. Finally there grew up a family of birds with no wings at all. Such was the great toothed diver, Hesperornis.

Yet swift and fierce as these birds were, many must have made a good meal for a plesiosaur. In Figure 123 we see a portion of a cliff and inland sea of Kansas. Hesperornis is facing a plesiosaur, but from the expression on their faces it is difficult to tell just what they are going to do. Perhaps they are merely talking about the latest non-stop flight of a pterodactyl, for several of these flying dragons are seen in the air. At the right and a little in the background a descendant of Archaeopteryx of Germany ventured near the surface to catch a small fish when a mosasaur jumped almost out of the water and nearly caught the ancient bird.

In these warm, shallow seas during the Cretaceous Period there grew millions upon millions of tiny shellfish called Foraminifera (Figure 124). Each shell was no larger than a grain of sand; so you can see how many many times the shells in the picture have been magnified. When the tiny animal is alive he floats through the water and is often eaten in large numbers by the small fish. When the Foraminifera escape being eaten alive and die a natural death, their shells drop to the bottom of the sea. The bottom of the ocean is full of tiny shells of all kinds. Apparently the warm, moist air and the quiet, clear, and shallow seas of the Cretaceous Period made these little Foraminifera very numerous, and instead of growing to be giants like many of the other fauna and

LIFE IN KANSAS IN THE CRETACEOUS PERIOD

Figure 123. On the right Ichthyosaurus has just failed to catch an ancient bird which ventured too near the water. Is that mosasaur about to eat Hesperornis? Or are they merely talking about the latest non-stop flight of a pterodactyl? Several of these dragons are flying around in the background. From *Water Reptiles of the Past and Present* by S. W. Williston of the University of Chicago.

flora, they simply grew great in numbers, piling their shells in heaps on the bottom of the seas. In the course of ages these masses of tiny shells became hardened, and

FORAMINIFERA

Figure 124. This is a picture of the way these shells look through a microscope when very greatly magnified.

now we call them chalk. The Romans called chalk *creta*, and so much chalk was made at this time that we call the period Cretaceous. You are probably wondering why we don't find oil in these masses of chalk. You remember that the little shellfish, in order to leave oil in the rock, must die in muddy water, so that the tiny globules of oil could unite with particles of mud and settle to the bottom. Where these Foraminifera lived the water was clear and the little globules of oil were washed away, so that only pure white shells accumulated at the bottom of the sea.

This period so marvelous for the development of the flora and fauna finally came to a terrible end. The crust of the earth, which had been quiet for so many millions of years, began to wrinkle. For most of the Cretaceous Period a long, narrow sea had covered the land that is now occupied by the Rocky Mountains from Alaska to Mexico. Where the Andes now are in South America there was a corresponding narrow sea. In the Jurassic Period we found the land was sinking in a narrow valley from Alaska to Mexico. You remember that we then suspected that this valley would make a weak point in the crust and that if ever the earth wrinkled again huge mountains might rise where this valley had been. And so they did at the end of the Cretaceous Period.

Due to the slow wrinkling of the crust of the earth, that long, narrow sea extending from Alaska to Mexico began to grow very shallow. As the ground rose here and there, the sea was cut off from the ocean. Then the bottom rose so that much dry land appeared and only lakes were left. Finally even these lakes disappeared. The land kept on rising for millions of years until finally the great Rocky Mountains stood where once Tylosaurus had ruled the sea. At the same time the Andes Mountains of South America were formed.

Before this happened, as we have already said, the Mississippi River flowed westward, perhaps over the land that is now called Arkansas, to the Pacific Ocean. When the Rocky Mountains rose the old river channel was blocked so that the water had to find a new outlet to the sea. Fortunately at the same time the land now called Louisiana and Mississippi sank a little and allowed the river to cut a channel to the Gulf of Mexico. Ever since then the great Mississippi Valley has sent all its waters to the Atlantic Ocean by way of the Gulf of Mexico. As the Mississippi River dug its channel deep down in the rock, it flowed through canyons with sides like cliffs. This was millions of years ago, and now the cliffs have been nearly all worn away so that the river often overflows its banks.

The map (Figure 125) shows how North America looked toward the end of the Cretaceous Period. In this period of rising land even the old Appalachian Mountains had risen again. On both the Atlantic and Pacific coasts the land extended into the ocean much farther than it does now. You also notice that Florida was very wide and was connected with Cuba.

With the growth of the mighty Rocky Mountains and the new growth of the old Appalachian Mountains, the air became so cold that there was a huge glacier in the

Courtesy of D. Van Nostrand Company

A MAP OF NORTH AMERICA IN THE CRETACEOUS PERIOD

Figure 125. The outline of this ancient continent has been somewhat modified from a drawing in *An Introduction to Historical Geology* by **W. J.** Miller, published by D. Van Nostrand Company. A modern outline map has been used as a basis to indicate the changes which have taken place. This outline map is published by Rand McNally and Company, by whose permission it has been reproduced.

southwestern part of Colorado. The inland seas and lakes were all dried up and drained by rivers which flowed through steep banks to the sea. As the inland seas disappeared and the moist warm air grew cold the huge ani-

Courtesy of the American Museum of Natural History

SIR HENRY DELABECHE'S DRAWING OF EXTINCT ANIMALS

Figure 126. Exaggerated as this picture undoubtedly is, it gives some idea of the terrible struggle for life that occurred at the close of the Age of Reptiles. After a quaint drawing in Buckland's *Curiosities of Natural History*. From *Animals of the Past* by F. A. Lucas, published by the American Museum of Natural History.

mals died. They couldn't stand cold weather. Even if they could have endured the ice and snow of winter, they would have starved to death, for they were set in their habits and could not learn new ways of getting food. Hesperornis had lost his wings and could only dive for

REPTILES

Figure 127. This is not a picture of life during the Age of Reptiles. It is a family of the present time. The two old fellows in the center are having a vigorous argument. Maybe they are talking about how times have changed and reptiles are no longer what they used to be. Imagine these lizards many times larger, and you will get some idea of life in the Cretaceous Period. From a photograph of an exhibit in the American Museum of Natural History, New York.

LIFE IN THE SEA IN THE CRETACEOUS PERIOD

Figure 128. Although the ocean on the shores of the continents was probably not always as crowded as this picture indicates, it gives some idea of sea life in the Cretaceous Period. From a drawing by Miss Alice B. Woodward in *Evolution in the Past* by H. R. Knipe, published by Herbert and Daniel, London.

fish. When the sea dried up, Hesperornis died, but fortunately left his skeleton in the mud for our museums. Little by little as the winters grew colder the giant dinosaurs and the great pterodactyls perished. As the end approached and the seas broke up into lakes, the fauna must have become crowded. Then there probably followed a fight for life such as the world had never seen before. It was a veritable war of giants. Perhaps the pictures (Figures 126, 127, and 128) give some idea of the struggle for existence that preceded the end of this glorious Age of Reptiles.

XV. EOCENE PERIOD

WE HAVE been on a long journey down through the ages. We started just as the great shooting stars ceased falling, and we saw the little germs appear in the warm oceans. We have watched our animals develop and successfully survive one crisis after another. Now we enter on a new group of periods. They are the last in this history, for we are approaching the end of our story. In this group of periods the great apes appear and man finally emerges as a branch of the order called primates. There are five of these geological periods, which are short in time compared with many other periods, but of momentous value to us. We speak of them all as "recent," and the first one is called "Dawn of the Recent," or in Greek, Eocene. It began perhaps 55 million years ago and lasted about 20 million years.

If you had really taken this imaginary journey, if you had been blindfolded at the end of the Cretaceous Period and if you had been allowed to look around you for the first time when the Eocene Period was well advanced, you would have been amazed at the change of scene—a new and almost modern world would have met you at every turn.

"The passage of time from the Cretaceous to the succeeding Eocene is shrouded in darkness; and the 'new dawn' follows a long night. It is as if the lights in a playhouse had been abruptly extinguished, and after a lapse had been restored, disclosing a stage crowded with new characters.

"The transition times were doubtless of long duration, and full of stirring events; but their archives for the most part have either been destroyed, or have yet to be discovered. The results, however, of what then took place are plain enough. There had been a great elimination of old forms of reptile and other life; and mammals had become dominant. Dinosaurs, herbivorous and carnivorous, had one and all vanished from the scene—iguanadonts . . . , stegosaurs with their battlemented backs and the rest of the fraternity. Old Triceratops with his thrice-horned head, and Elizabethan frill, seems to have held out as long as any; but fortune failed him at last. In short the old reptile nobility, unable to march with the times, had been swept away. Nor had ichthyosaurs, plesiosaurs, mosasaurs, and flying lizards fared any better. They had all quitted the stage never to return." So writes H. R. Knipe in his book, *Evolution in the Past*.

While we know very little about the early part of the Eocene Period, we do know that the many mammals that now appear must have been developing during the latter part of the Cretaceous, but up to the present time their remains have not been found. Perhaps it was due to the disappearance of the large reptiles that the small mammals "which couldn't look a reptile in the face" developed into goodly-sized animals of a number of varieties, which ultimately became our familiar horses, bears, rats, cows. lions, apes, and even men.

North America (Figure 129) must have been a beautiful country during this Dawn of the Recent. The mountains along the Pacific coast were worn into rounded hills. The rushing torrents with rapids and waterfalls had disappeared. To be sure, there were many volcanoes in the States of Oregon and Washington, but for the most part North America was at peace with the interior of the earth, and volcanic eruptions and earthquakes were rare. The great Appalachian Mountains were rapidly crumbling away, and before the end of the period they had become gracefully curved low hills, covered with forests and green food for the new mammals.

The great rivers that we know so well were not far from their present locations. The Colorado, Snake, and Columbia Rivers of the west coast drained their countries of the surplus rainfall much as they do today. In the east there was the St. Lawrence River which flowed over land that has now sunk below the Atlantic Ocean, for the land through which the river flowed was more than 1,000 feet higher above the ocean than at present. There was dry land where the fishermen now catch codfish on the Grand

Courtesy of D. Van Nostrand Company

A MAP OF NORTH AMERICA IN THE EOCENE PERIOD

Figure 129. Through the courtesy of Rand McNally and Company one of their outline maps has been printed over the land area of the Eocene Period in order to indicate some of the changes which have taken place. The outlines of the ancient continent have been taken from a drawing in *An Introduction to Historical Geology* by W. J. Miller, published by D. Van Nostrand Company.

Banks. You can even now see where this ancient St. Lawrence River flowed by looking at the maps that give the depths of the ocean for the region just south of Newfoundland. The Connecticut and Hudson Rivers flowed through valleys that closely resemble their channels of today, except that the mouths of these rivers were at points that are now far out to sea; for since this period the land has sunk and allowed the ocean to flood a portion of these ancient river channels. The Hudson River flowed through a deep canyon and reached the sea at a place now under several hundred feet of water.

We found that during the last period the land now occupied by Mississippi and Louisiana had sunk enough to enable the Mississippi River to cut a new channel between deep canyon walls to the Gulf of Mexico. During the Eocene Period the sinking of the southern part of the Mississippi valley continued until the Gulf of Mexico flowed over this sunken land as far north as where the Ohio River now flows into the Mississippi River. Then for some unknown reason the land began to rise again until now the Mississippi River flows into the Gulf of Mexico much as it did at the end of the Cretaceous Period.

If a Californian had wandered through the Eocene woodlands he would have felt very much at home, for the great sequoia trees made stately forests in Canada as well as in the country now occupied by the Rocky Mountains. These wonderful trees—sometimes over 300 feet high and fifteen to twenty feet in diameter—live to be several thousand years old. "I never saw a 'big tree' that had died a natural death; barring accidents they seem to be immortal, being exempt from all the diseases that afflict and kill other trees. Unless destroyed by man, they live on indefinitely until burned, smashed by lightning or cast down by storms or by the giving way of the ground on which they stand." John Muir is thus quoted by C. Schuchert in *Historical Geology*. In the Eocene Period they grew from Spitzbergen within the Arctic Circle to the middle of Italy. They grew in China as well as over most of North America. They are among the few great giants of the past living today. Perhaps they are the biggest living things that have grown on the earth. California is their guardian, for there only have they survived (Figure 78).

A curious feature of those days was the unusual variety of trees which grew in the same forest. Nowadays an oak tree will grow only where the air is cold enough to kill a banana tree. Yet oak, banana, fig, and breadfruit trees grew side by side on the coast of North America. Now the breadfruit tree is found only in the tropics.

The world had fewer bleak and ice-cold countries in those Eocene days. Magnolia trees and delicate ferns grew along the Yukon River in Alaska. In Greenland there were forests of cypress trees like those now found in the swamps of the southern states, cedars, sycamores, magnolias, willows, poplars, bayberries, elm trees, tulip trees, oaks, maples, birches, ash, hazelnut trees, sequoias, sumacs, plum trees, persimmon trees and grape vines. The shores of the country we now call southern England were full of crocodiles and huge water snakes, and forests of palm trees flourished on the land. Birds with bills notched like a saw flew over the Thames River where London has since been built.

In Eocene days the Mississippi River was a northern stream, for its mouth was near St. Louis, where now we have snow in winter. However, this Eocene Mississippi River had dense tropical foliage on its banks the year round (Figure 130).

For the first time the flora had begun to show color on a large scale, for the flowering plants now predominated in the plains and forests. Heretofore, ferns, evergreens, and those queer Carboniferous trees had been the prevailing flora.

Probably also the birds had brilliant plumage in this period, for the primitive ancestors of many of our well-known birds lived during the approximate 20 million years of the Dawn of the Recent. Here is a list of a few of the birds which can trace their family tree back to the Eocene: albatross, goose, crane, flamingo, stork, owl, woodpecker, swift, quail, nuthatch, starling, lark, and warbler.

If these birds should have a convention to discuss the progress of their race and perhaps to make plans for peace and goodwill among birds, there would be some sorrow-

Courtesy of Edward W. Berry

THE BANKS OF THE MISSISSIPPI RIVER IN THE EOCENE PERIOD

Figure 130. "Nipa palms on a tidal flat in the Philippine Islands. Similar palms grew in the estuaries of the late lower Eocene embayment." From *Romance of Collecting Fossil Plants* by Edward W. Berry of Johns Hopkins University, published in *Natural History* (American Museum of Natural History).

ful remarks about the disappearance of Diatrima (Figure 131). The Diatrima in this dawn period grew prosperous, huge, and muscular. Like Hesperornis (Figure 122) in the Cretaceous Period, he had lost the art of

Courtesy of the American Museum of Natural History

DIATRIMA

Figure 131. The giant Eocene bird of North America. From a drawing by E. S. Christman at the American Museum of Natural History.

flying. He stalked through the forests and over the plains of North America, killing and eating small animals. The Diatrima found it was easy enough to grow fat and big when all other animals were small and slow. Perhaps it was this satisfied feeling that caused his downfall, for we shall soon see that some of the animals grew swift and savage as tigers and began eating Diatrima until finally Diatrima existed no more.

Through this veritable Garden of Eden, the primi-

LEAF OF FAN-PALM

Figure 132. It would have been possible to make palm-leaf fans four feet wide if you had lived in New Mexico during the Eocene Period. This is a picture, much reduced, of a fossil palm leaf which got caught in the Eocene mud about 40 million years ago. From *Plants of the Past* by F. H. Knowlton of Princeton University.

tive mammals now roamed almost without fear; for their chief enemies, the giant reptiles, had perished. Perhaps only Diatrima was dangerous, and he was rare. To be sure, there were alligators and large water snakes, and the ocean was full of sharks; but why should the mammal fear these water creatures as he ran through the forests of tall sequoias and oaks and perhaps rested in the shade of a four-foot palm leaf? (Figure 132.) He prospered greatly and grew and multiplied. We call him a primitive mammal because he was the oldest large mammal that has been discovered. He was neither dog, horse, cat,

Courtesy of the American Museum of Natural History

ARCHAIC MAMMALS

Figure 133. After the disappearance of the giant reptiles, these primitive mammals enjoyed the freedom and the safety of the early Eocene. Pantalambda is on the left and Coryphodon on the right. From models in the American Museum of Natural History.

nor elephant. He was just a plain mammal and in some ways resembled all those animals, of which he is the common ancestor (Figure 133).

Although this wonderful Eocene world was theirs and although there was hardly an enemy to disturb their slumbers, yet the archaic mammals began killing and eating each other as the great reptiles had done before them. We inherit this tendency even to the present day, for

PATRIOFELIS

Figure 134. He wants that alligator, but he doesn't dare go into the water after him. A few million years later his collateral descendants became the wonderful saber-tooth tigers. From a painting by C. R. Knight under the direction of H. F. Osborn of the American Museum of Natural History.

mankind is supreme with hardly an enemy to disturb his slumbers; yet he is forever making war upon his fellow man and killing him by the thousand. These early meat-eaters are called creodonts. Patriofelis was a prominent

Courtesy of the American Museum of Natural History

PHENOCODUS, A COUSIN OF THE HORSE'S ANCESTOR

Figure 135. Would the horse of today recognize his early Eocene ancestor? Phenocodus' family name was Condylarth, and some of his descendants became rhinoceroses. After a painting by C. R. Knight under the direction of H. F. Osborn at the American Museum of Natural History.

member of this group (Figure 134). If he was not the direct ancestor of the modern tiger he must at least have been a great-uncle.

Some of the archaic ones gave proof that it is possible to be progressive, change ways of living, and yet not hurt one's fellow mammals. When this group came out of their hiding-places after the terrible dinosaurs had perished, they roamed through the forests and developed a taste for plants and leaves instead of insects and fruit. They were a peaceful crowd which would rather run than fight. Patriofelis and his gang soon gave them so much practice in running that they developed wonderful speed. Phenacodus (Figure 135) was the founder of his family and became the ancestor of a very famous mammal—the horse.

Eohippus, the descendant of Phenacodus, was the first primitive horse—no larger than a small dog. Dawn-horse he is sometimes called, for that is the meaning of the Greek word Eohippus (Figure 136). The familiar hoof is missing, for in those Eocene days he ran on four toes, with a fifth toe that didn't quite touch the ground. Perhaps Patriofelis frightened him so badly that in his haste to escape he didn't have time to get all five toes on the ground. Those of the little dawn-horses that were slow soon met with a terrible fate (Figure 137). Therefore, only those horses survived which could run like mad and escape the rapidly developing tigers, for the tigers, too, had to live. The faster the plant-eaters ran, the quicker the meateaters became in springing on their prey unexpectedly. So the contest continued for millions of years, as it has been doing in the world of fauna ever since one group of cells declared war on another and ate them alive. The slow and weak perished miserably, and from

Courtesy of the American Museum of Natural History

EOHIPPUS

Figure 136. The dawn-horse of the early part of the Eocene. After a drawing by C. R. Knight at the American Museum of Natural History.

"The beasts, four-toed and three, move far more fleet
Than any Coryphodon. Indeed their feet
To suit their mode of life compact have grown,
And on some toes but little weight is thrown.
Perchance, ill-armed, they find in flight there lies
The way most safe to treat their enemies:
And tip-toeing off for vigilance and speed,
They will in time their side-toes scarcely need.
Indeed these by degrees will disappear,
Or be but stunted forms of what they were;
For life will ever slowly tend to lose
All nature's gifts, which are not put to use.
What may these creatures fleet and fox-sized be,
That little-armed, may find it best to flee
Than face and fight a well-armed enemy?
Mixed forms they are; yet maybe hold the place
Of founders humble of the equine race."

From *Nebula to Man* by H. R. Knipe, published by J. M. Dent and Sons, Ltd., London.

EOHIPPUS DID NOT RUN FAST ENOUGH

Figure 137. A primitive Eocene tiger Oxyaena has begun that long contest with the horse that was destined to last for millions of years. In the end the tiger grew stronger and the horse grew faster. After a painting by C. R. Knight, made under the direction of H. F. Osborn for the American Museum of Natural History.

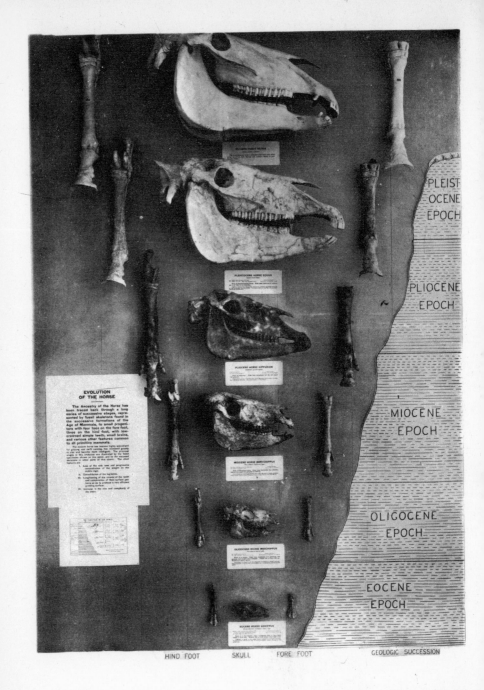

SKELETON DEVELOPMENT OF THE HORSE'S FOOT AND HEAD

Figure 138. After an exhibit in the American Museum of Natural History. From *Evolution of the Horse* by W. D. Matthew and S. H. Chubb.

these bloody scenes emerged the swift horse and the savage tiger of our own day.

The effort to escape from Patriofelis and his successors, the lions, tigers, and leopards, has had a curious effect on the shape of the horse's foot. We have already found that early in the Eocene, the little dawn-horse Eohippus was scampering through the forests on four toes. When his descendants were forced to run faster by the increasing power of the cat gang, they depended more and more on the middle toe, and the other four toes were used less and less. In this world what is not used soon disappears, and thus the other toes gradually vanished and the one big center toe took their place. We now call this big toe the horse's hoof. In Figure 138 you can follow this change in the skeleton of the foot through the various ages to the present time. Thus fright played a large part in turning five toes into a hoof—perhaps we might call it the shell-shock of those early days.

As we have already found, there are often several reasons why certain events have taken place, and the change in the shape of the horse's foot may be another example. We shall find later that in subsequent periods the air grew colder and many of the forests became grassy plains. In order to get food, perhaps the horse was obliged to run on the plains and learn to eat grass. Therefore he didn't need the paws that he had used in climbing over the fallen trees of the forest (Figure 139).

When food is abundant animals usually grow larger.

EOCENE PERIOD

The larger animals have an advantage, for they can protect themselves better than their smaller companions. The horse was no exception to this rule. On the plains he found plenty of food, and for tens of millions of years he grew steadily larger and swifter.

Even before the Eocene Period had closed, this dawn-horse had made progress and gave promise of his future

Courtesy of F. B. Loomis, Geological Department, Amherst College

EVOLUTION OF THE HORSE

Figure 139. After 50 million years the descendant of the little Eohippus on the left of the line has become the magnificent horse of today at the right of the line. Now the gasoline engine is taking the horse's place. So evolution may be as relentless for the horse as it was for the dinosaur. From an exhibit at the Museum at Amherst College (photograph by W. E. Corbin).

greatness. Orohippus is the name of the horse that represents this second stage (Figure 140).

During all this time one branch of the primitive mammals continued to live on fruit and insects. Like Dromatherium (Figure 91) in the Triassic Period, these mammals were small and found it safer to spend most of their time in the trees. They were the founders of our branch of the animal world, for they were primitive primates. Notharctus of Wyoming (Figure 141) is often regarded

[260]

OROHIPPUS

Figure 140. During the latter part of the Eocene Period the horse had become a little larger and swifter. We call the leader of this group Orohippus. In the picture he is seen leading the group to drink. They are keeping at a safe distance from the large animals across the stream, which is in the country we now call Wyoming. There is an active volcano in the distance. After a painting by C. R. Knight, made under the direction of H. F. Osborn.

"And though their feet four toes and three possess,
Yet on one toe of each foot most they press,
And outer toes are slowly growing less."

From *Nebula to Man* by H. R. Knipe, published by J. M. Dent and Sons, Ltd., London.

as the leading North American member of this group. It is difficult to trace any family likeness, for he does not look much like any man we ever saw. Yet he must have been a bright little animal during those Eocene years, for some of the descendants of his generation became the rulers of the earth. It may be that that primate branch

Courtesy of The Macmillan Company

NOTHARCTUS

Figure 141. A member of one of the "first families" of Wyoming in the Eocene days. From some of his remote cousins we are probably descended. Notharctus was perhaps a yard long if we include his tail. After a drawing by C. R. Knight for *Age of Mammals* by H. F. Osborn of the American Museum of Natural History.

of the archaic mammal race possessed curiosity, which is perhaps the best characteristic a primate can have, for in satisfying curiosity his knowledge grows, and so, and only so, he learns new ways of living.

At first these little mammals placed all their faith in their noses. They learned to detect a lurking enemy by his smell. Those who were not so good at smelling usually had very unfortunate experiences when the big meat-eating dinosaurs shook the land as they sprang on their victims. When, however, Notharctus was in a tree, he had less use for that fine nose he had inherited. No matter

Courtesy of W. B. Scott

ANAPTOMORPHUS

Figure 142. Evidently this little fellow, a cousin of our Eocene ancestors, depended less upon his nose and more upon his eyes. He is described in *History of Land Mammals in the Western Hemisphere* by W. B. Scott of Princeton University, published by The Macmillan Company.

how near the enemy might be, so long as he was not on Notharctus' tree, the little primate would be safe, at least for the time being. Therefore, good eyes became more important to these tree-living animals than good noses. Thus the sharp-eyed primates had a better chance to survive and bring up a family of little primates than the sharp-nosed smellers. Also in jumping from limb to limb, his nose did him very little service; in fact it was rather in the way, but his eyesight was absolutely essential.

TARSIUS

Figure 143. He lives in the East Indies and still closely resembles his Eocene ancestor. He looks like a cousin of ours, and he is. From *Evolution of the Vertebrates* by Alfred S. Romer in the *Nature of the World and of Man.*

After millions of years this changed the primate's face as much as running away from tigers had changed the horse's foot (Anaptomorphus, Figure 142).

Some little primates got as far as this first change in their faces, and then they stopped developing. We have met with this curious thing ever since we began to explore the ancient periods of this earth. You remember how useful this feature of animal life has been, for we found how the very ancient birds looked by examining the hoat-

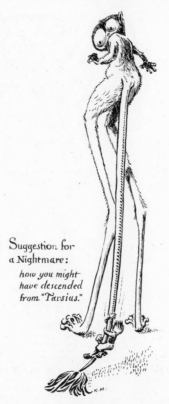

Suggestion for
a Nightmare:
*how you might
have descended
from "Tarsius."*

zins (Figure 95), which are living in South America and have apparently changed hardly at all from the very early times. Now we find in the East Indies a little tree-living mammal that has changed little from the time when his Eocene ancestors began to develop their eyes and to ignore their noses. His name is Tarsius (Figure 143), and with Notharctus and Anaptomorphus his portrait should hang in our dining-rooms.

Now for the first time you can begin to see our family likeness. Thus in the 20 million years of the Eocene Period the first primitive human face appeared.

XVI. OLIGOCENE PERIOD

In order that we may understand the names that have been given to the remaining four periods in the earth's history, let us learn them all now so that by arranging them in their proper sequence we can find their true meaning. The latest period, the one from which we are now emerging, is called the "Most Recent" or Pleistocene. It began about 1 million years ago. Previous to Pleistocene came Pliocene ("More Recent"), which commenced about 7 million years ago and lasted about 6 million years. Then as we go back in time we come to the "Less Recent" or Miocene. The periods are growing longer as they grow more ancient, for the Miocene began perhaps 19 million years ago and lasted for approximately 12 million years.

Finally we come to the Oligocene Period, the subject of this chapter. Translated, the name means "Little of the Recent." It began about 35 million years ago and lasted probably at least 16 million years.

No stirring events marked this period; no large mountain ranges rose to the clouds, no new and strange race of animals appeared, and also no very well-known rulers of the earth disappeared. Life on land and in the sea and air continued to develop during the Oligocene much as it had in the preceding Eocene. You remember that during the Eocene the mountains were crumbling away and the air was growing warm and moist. The Oligocene gave the earth 16 million more years in which to carry on this work, for during the Oligocene the wearing away of the hills continued until the land was almost a plain (peneplain) and not much above the ocean.

In outline, North America began to have a more modern appearance (Figure 144). Greenland began to separate from Canada, but the east coast was still as far out to sea as it was in the Eocene. That rising of the land in the lower Mississippi valley continued so that by the middle of the Oligocene Period the great river flowed into the Gulf of Mexico at a point not far from the northern boundary of Louisiana. Florida, as you can see from the map, was merely a small island, for nearly all of that peninsula was under water as well as the southern parts of Alabama, Mississippi, and Georgia. The West Indies, which in the Eocene had consisted of one extensive island, had disappeared entirely beneath the waves. So also had Yucatan, and Panama, if it had existed, would not have needed a canal, for North and South America were widely separated during this period. The sharks, the only cruising submarines in those days, freely swam from ocean to ocean.

On the west coast, where the entrance to the Gulf of

Courtesy of D. Van Nostrand Company

A MAP OF NORTH AMERICA IN THE OLIGOCENE PERIOD

Figure 144. The contours of the Oligocene continent have been taken with some modification from a drawing in *An Introduction to Historical Geology*, by W.J. Miller, published by D. Van Nostrand Company. A modern outline map has been reproduced through the courtesy of the publishers, Rand McNally and Company.

OLIGOCENE PERIOD

California now lies, the land had begun to sink and to be slowly, very slowly, flooded by the sea. Thus that gulf, so clearly shown in our geographies, began to take its present shape in the Oligocene Period. California had some strange land to its west—a land doomed eventually to sink beneath the sea. The States of Oregon and Washington had a tempestuous prehistoric past, for during the 34 million years of the Oligocene, Miocene, and Pliocene Periods, volcanoes made the night skies lurid and covered the land with ashes and streams of molten lava.

British Columbia, like the eastern coast of North America, extended far into the ocean. Like that land to the west of California, this also sank into the depths of the sea, but so slowly that in the remaining 35 million years of the earth's history it has not entirely disappeared. That coast is full of islands and partly submerged valleys which are the remnants of its greater past. Finally, we know that Alaska, a little larger than now, was a continuous land bridge between North America and Asia.

The world was like a great greenhouse during the Oligocene Period. Warm, moist air covered the low hills and dense forests (Figure 145). When the sun was low in the southern skies and there were long, dark nights in the north, there must have been tremendous storms which swept over North America from west to east—cyclones of hurricane force. Also this hot air overburdened with little globules of water probably produced thunderstorms of gigantic proportions. Those corridors, 100 feet high, between the great sequoia trees echoed with the peals of Oligocene thunder and were illuminated with flashes of lightning far surpassing any in our experience.

SCENE IN EUROPE IN THE OLIGOCENE

Figure 145. No cold north winds from Greenland's icy mountains could bring frost to this luxuriant growth, for there existed neither ice nor high mountains to disturb this forest. Nearly all the land in the world was low, with well-rounded hills, and covered with hot moist air. Drawn by E. P. Bucknall for *Evolution of the Past*, by H. R. Knipe, published by Herbert and Daniel, London.

In these forests and over the plains, in clear weather and in stormy weather, the great age-long contest continued—the survival of the fittest. The meat-eating creodonts were hard pressed, for some rivals which sprang more savagely to the attack had invaded North America.

[271]

They came possibly from Asia across that land bridge of Alaska. Apparently, many of the meat-eaters had developed more rapidly in Asia, for they treated the native

Courtesy of W. B. Scott

HYENODON HORRIDUS

Figure 146. The last of his race. He represents the old-fashioned meat-eaters called creodonts. They couldn't compete with the tigers and bear-dogs. After gaining a poor living by eating dead animals they perished in the struggle for existence. From *History of Land Mammals in the Western Hemisphere* by W. B. Scott of Princeton University, published by The Macmillan Company.

creodonts as ruthlessly as the white men from Europe later treated the native Indians. One of the last creodonts to yield to the new supremacy was *Hyenodon horridus* (Figure 146).

A PRIMITIVE OLIGOCENE CAT, DINICTIS

Figure 147. It may be that Dinictis represents an intermediate stage between the savage meat-eating creodont and the magnificent and overwhelming saber-toothed tiger. Yet Dinictis survived for some time and was even a contemporary of Hoplophoneus. From a painting by C. R. Knight, under the direction of H. F. Osborn.

OLIGOCENE PERIOD

The cat family was now supreme; it was the royal family of the sequoia forests. Dinictis (Figure 147) was perhaps the first to display modern lines and to develop

Courtesy of the American Museum of Natural History

AN OLIGOCENE SABER-TOOTH TIGER, HOPLOPHONEUS

Figure 148. The descendants of this Oligocene cat became the famous saber-tooth tigers that terrified the early primates. Like *Tyrannosaurus rex* all animals served as food for his ravenous jaws. They did one good thing, however; they made the horse learn how to run. From a drawing by C. R. Knight.

that athletic jump that has made the family famous. However, he was soon surpassed by his cousin Hoplophoneus (Figure 148), who began to display a gleaming pair of ivory teeth that must have been the envy as well as the terror of the Oligocene fauna.

While the tigers were growing larger and receiving re-inforcements from other continents, the horses weren't by any means asleep in the sunlight, for those that were soon met with a tragic death. You remember that the horse was a peaceful mammal and believed in flight when tigers were around. The exercise forced on him by Dinictis and Hoplophoneus made him larger and swifter. Mesohippus (Figure 149) is the leader of these Oligocene horses. More and more Mesohippus relied on that middle toe, which slowly developed into a hoof.

Not all the meat-eaters had developed into lions and tigers, the animals we call the cat family. During the Oligocene Period some descendants of the creodonts de-veloped family traits of their own, and in the late Oligo-cene they produced a meat-eater which is, perhaps, the earliest representative of the dog family. His name is Cynodictis (Figure 150), and he is often called the ances-tor of the fox.

It is a long time now since we have explored the depths of the ocean. Before the Dawn of the Recent it was full of mosasaurs, plesiosaurs, ichthyosaurs, chelonians, and sharks. In the Oligocene, if we had been guests of Nep-tune, we should have found only two large monsters: whales and sharks.

One of these marine creatures was a mammal which had been forced to undertake a seafaring life. We now call him a whale, and he has been so long in the water that he looks for all the world like a fish. Once upon a time his ancestors ran around on the land, for he is descended

MESOHIPPUS

Figure 149. A swift light-limbed three-toed horse that lived in North America during the first part of the Oligocene Period. Watching this horse is the primitive tiger Dinictis. After a drawing by C. R. Knight in the American Museum of Natural History. From *Age of Mammals* by H. F. Osborn.

from those little primitive mammals that used to hide from dinosaurs (Figure 109) in the Jurassic and Cretaceous Periods. You recall that many times in the past, land animals have been forced into the ocean by hunger or by fear, or perhaps by both. Some reptiles took up the fisherman's life and became ichthyosaurs and mosasaurs. Even the great bird Hesperornis (Figure 122) gave up

Courtesy of W. B. Scott

AN ANCESTOR OF THE FOX, CYNODICTIS

Figure 150. Perhaps this meat-eater, the descendant of some creodont, was the ancestor of the fox. Cynodictis lived during the last part of the Oligocene Period. From *History of Land Mammals in the Western Hemisphere* by W. B. Scott of Princeton University, published by The Macmillan Company.

flying and earned his living by diving and swimming. So some of the mammals, when they were crowded off the land, showed that they too could adopt not only an amphibian but even a fish's life. The mammal's paws gradually turned into fins in exactly the same way and for exactly the same reasons that had long before changed the reptile's feet into fins (Figure 81).

The first primitive whale was a queer-looking animal, and he also had a strange name, Zeuglodon (Figure 151). In the course of time, however, he became more compact and a much faster swimmer. At least, those that didn't change in this way became food for sharks, so that after millions of years the modern whale was developed.

It is claimed that sharks are the brightest of fishes. Such superiority seems probable, for we have found that in all ages animals that earned their food by killing those of about their own size were usually the ablest and brightest of their contemporaries. Combat on nearly equal terms seems to sharpen the wits of all fauna. It is because in so dangerous an occupation only those survive who can think quickly. However, bright as a shark may be in comparison with a codfish, he certainly cannot boast of any great intellectual achievement. Roaming the forests and plains has produced more brains than flying in the air or swimming in the sea, for neither birds nor insects can compete with the products of the forests —the mammals, among whom the primates take first place.

If you had again accepted Neptune's invitation to visit the vast stretches of warm water in the Oligocene, you would have been convinced that the sharks were destined to be undisputed rulers of the sea. They had grown to an unheard-of size, and their ferocity must have been the

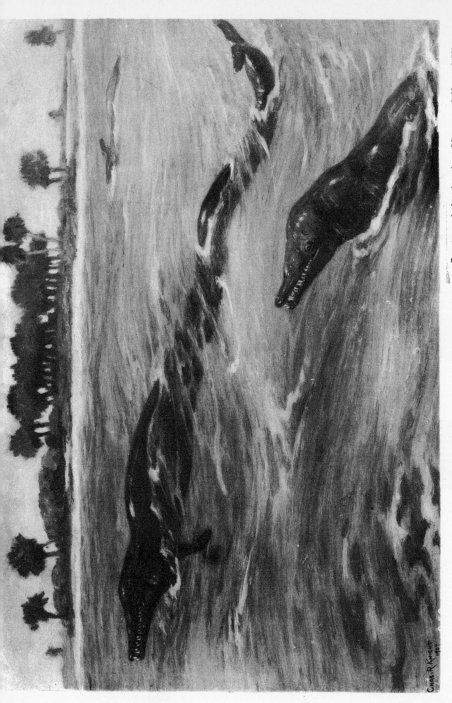

ZEUGLODON

Figure 151. A primitive whale that in the Oligocene Period swam in the water that is now called the Gulf of Mexico
A whaler in those days might wonder whether he were hunting sea-serpents or whales. After a drawing by C. R.
Knight.

equal of that of *Tyrannosaurus rex* (Figure 111). Carcharodon (Figure 152) was the name of this shark, and

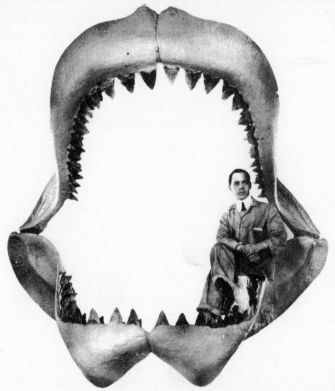

Courtesy of the American Museum of Natural History

CARCHARODON, A GIANT OLIGOCENE SHARK

Figure 152. Next to a California sequoia tree, it may be that Carcharodon
was the largest living thing that has ever grown upon the earth. As
long as a twelve-story building is high, this monster ruled the seas.
After a photograph of an exhibit at the American Museum of Natural
History.

he was the terror of all that came within the reach of his
huge jaws. His family began its career in the Eocene

Period and formed probably Neptune's ablest admirals of the navy until well into the Miocene.

"Once fairly started in life these huge sharks spread themselves throughout the warm seas of the world, for there was none might stand before them and say nay. They swarmed everywhere that the water was sufficiently warm, for their teeth occur in . . . strata in many parts of the world. . . . And then they perished, perished as utterly as did the hosts of Sennacherib. Why? We do not know. Did they devour everything large enough to be eaten . . . and then fall to eating one another? Again we do not know. But perish they did, while the smaller white shark, which came into being at the same time, still lives, as if to emphasize the fact that it is best not to overdo things and that in the long run the victory is not always with the largest," says F. A. Lucas in his delightful little book, *Animals of the Past*.

We have reserved for the last the next stage in our own family history, for we now have before us a fairly good picture of Oligocene geography, climate, and life in forest and sea. For 16 million years our family of primates lived in this beautiful country of stately forests and brilliant thunderstorms, but amid a turmoil of combat and sudden death. It is no wonder that like Tarsius they continued to live in the trees and to eat fruit and insects as their ancestors had done for tens of millions of years. As those early primates swung from branch to branch over the snarling, shrieking death-struggle that ever and again occurred far down among the ferns and roots of the tree, they little realized that the fear which kept them in the tree was some day to make them the rulers of the world. We have already found how fear helped to give the horse his hoof and also perhaps made him one of the fastest animals that ever ran on four feet. Now we find that the fear that may have kept the primates in the tree, thereby turned their forepaws into two hands with four fingers and a thumb. To live in a tree you must have good grasping power. If a primate failed to have such power by inheritance, or if through carelessness he failed to use it, he must sometimes fall, and then all too often his next journey was into the stomach of Hoplophoneus. Thus the five toes became five fingers for the same reason that a fish's fin had become a foot in the Devonian Period (Figure 39), 300 million years before.

Life all over the world was much the same as in North America, but some of the animals in Asia were better developed. We have already found that a few of the descendants of the meat-eating Asiatic creodonts had migrated to North America, where they had proved to be better fighters than the natives. In the same way the primates were possibly more progressive in Asia than elsewhere. It may have been because they originated there. Therefore, for our own family history we must turn to Asia and probably to that part of the country that is now called the Gobi Desert. In those Oligocene days it was covered with a dense forest including many giant sequoias. The tribes of little animals like Notharctus and later the tribe like Tarsius were probably there, for these little creatures apparently had spread far and wide.

The primates that looked like Tarsius had better eyes than the family of Notharctus, for Notharctus, like many animals, had an eye on each side of his head, very much like a squirrel. After millions of years, however, the primates like Tarsius developed a face, so that they could see the same object with both eyes at the same time. Now the descendants of the Tarsius tribe in Gobi were still brighter-eyed. The leader of this new group of well-formed primates is called Propliopithecus (Figure 153). After millions of years of experience he had developed a bigger brain than his ancestors who resembled Tarsius. The ability to hold an object in his hand and look at it with both eyes, probably developed that most valuable of all traits, curiosity. The more he wanted to know, the more he learned, until now some of the descendants of Propliopithecus or his contemporaries know about radio, what the stars are made of, and even the origin and story of the earth.

Although the early primates were a peaceful lot, they must have had at least some differences of opinion in those 16 million Oligocene years; for during that period one group after another left the family of Propliopithecus and started a little tree-living community of their own. Apparently these bloodless revolutions were caused by the differences between the progressives and the conservatives. As the primate population grew and the trees got crowded it became even harder to get enough to eat.

Courtesy of the New York Zoölogical Society

PROPLIOPITHECUS AS REPRESENTED BY HIS GRANDCHILD
THE GIBBON

Figure 153. The Gibbon and we have old Grandfather Propliopithecus for a common ancestor, and the Gibbon, we are told, has retained a very strong family likeness. So the Gibbon posed for this picture, which also should be hung in our ancestral gallery. After a photograph by E. R. Sanborn of the New York Zoölogical Society.

Then a primate could choose between two ways of living: he could either move off into a more distant forest and continue to live as his ancestors had done, or he could stay where he was and learn new and better ways of getting food. Probably no primate ever sat on a limb and pondered the choice. As the forests became crowded each primate every day did the best he could to get his daily food and bring up his family of little primates. Some just naturally wandered farther and farther away, while others developed better ways of getting food and protecting their families and stayed nearer home.

The first to leave home and travel far were those that came to North America and then went on to South America. It was a long journey, and it took millions of years to travel from the old homestead in Gobi. The descendants of these early travelers to the New World are living still in South America, and we call them monkeys. They represent a very conservative branch of our family. They have probably changed neither their way of living nor even the expression of their faces very much since their ancestors separated from the family of primates in those far-off days in Gobi.

Every group seems to have a limit beyond which it cannot develop. This is true even of individuals. We can learn to run fast, and as we practice more we run faster; yet try as hard as we may, we never can run as fast as some of our playmates. Some of us can learn arithmetic and geometry, and we have even passed our examination in algebra; but we know in our hearts that we don't understand algebra and that we never will, because our mathematical mind could comprehend no more than geometry. So we find that all athletes, all mathematicians, and all musicians have a limit beyond which they can never go. This is more than a primate characteristic; it is a fauna characteristic, for it pervades the life of the world.

We find that, after the New World monkeys left, the primates progressed greatly until they were spending some time on the ground and were walking erect on their hind legs. The great grassy plains that encroached on the forests during the Oligocene Period probably forced these primates to seek at least a portion of their food on the ground.

The primates had become so expert that they no longer needed a tail to help them swing from limb to limb and therefore, like the unused toes in the foot of Eohippus, the tails began to disappear. At this point a large group met their limit. They could stand this modern progress no longer and ever after continued to live at this stage in their development. They are living today, and we call them gibbons. They now inhabit the southeastern part of Asia and the East Indies. These gibbons, erect and spry, probably closely resemble old Grandfather Propliopithecus.

The next group that could not stand the intellectual strain of remaining a member of the ancient but progressive family, traveled far to the west and eventually came to Africa. We call them Old World monkeys. Colobus

Courtesy of Wide World Photos

COLOBUS

Figure 154. His family were progressives in the land of Gobi; but late in the Oligocene Period, Colobus became a conservative. He has now become an Old World monkey, and is so conservative that he is sometimes called a "living fossil." After a photograph by Hilda Hempl Heller. From the New York *Times*.

(Figure 154) is a good example. Probably because he left the ancestral country later, he looks a little more intelligent than the gibbons. However, the family of Colobus had reached their limit; apparently they were proud of having become Old World monkeys, and monkeys they have been ever since.

Thus it took the 16 million years of the Oligocene Period for the family of Propliopithecus to develop from the ability of a Tarsius to the intelligence of a New World monkey, to that of a gibbon, and finally to the comparatively high standing of the Old World monkey, Colobus.

TRACES of a great-great-great

XVII. MIOCENE PERIOD

THE Miocene Period, meaning "Less Recent," began about 19 million years ago and lasted perhaps 12 million years. Thus it came down to within a few million years of our own time. When we consider the long spaces of time that we have been using, it would seem as if a period that ended only about 7 million years ago might be considered almost historical. However, we must remember that there is a vast difference between a few thousand and a few million years, and a great many very important events took place in the remaining 7 million years.

It was during the 12 million years of the Miocene that modern life began to develop the shapes and habits that are familiar to us. One reason for this change was the cooler weather that began toward the end of the period. During a large part of the time, however, that luxuriant greenhouse life continued.

We know a great deal about the trees and insects of the Miocene Age because of those very useful volcanoes. Nothing can be so destructive as a volcano, except perhaps the subsidence of a large section of land beneath the ocean. Yet the volcanoes have preserved for us many interesting things from the past, such as the forests of fossil trees in the Yellowstone National Park and the wonderful ruins of Pompeii. In this period the volcanoes did a third convenient thing—they buried with ashes an ancient lake called Lake Florissant, and it was done so

FOSSIL INSECT

Figure 155. Before being buried by volcanic ashes this insect used to hover over the water of Lake Florissant. From a photograph of an exhibit in the American Museum of Natural History.

quickly that thousands of insects (Figure 155) and leaves and flowers were caught in the mud, pressed flat, and preserved for us as fossils. Therefore we know that there grew in the western part of the country in the Miocene such trees and plants as alders, oaks, narrow-leafed cottonwoods, pines, wild roses, thistles, asters, sumach

(Figure 156), and Virginia creepers. Then there were flora that now grow only in warm countries, such as holly, smoke tree, sweet gum, and persimmon. The great sequoia forests still covered the land, for it was during this period that there grew and were destroyed those fifteen fossil forests of the Yellowstone National Park (Figure 26).

Europe was much like America in those days. It consisted of low, flat hills and many shallow inland seas. At the beginning of the Miocene there were no snow-capped Alps. The general appearance of the flora of mid-Europe was probably much as it was on the shores of Lake Florissant in Colorado. Figure 157 is a scene in the land now called Switzerland before the earth wrinkled and made mountains and glaciers.

For a long time the Mediterranean Sea had been much larger than it is now. For millions of years certain little creatures flourished in this warm and shallow body of water. They are called nummalites because they are so round and flat that they resemble the Roman coin *nummulus.* In some places these shells had accumulated until the deposits were 1,000 feet thick and after millions of years were pressed into rock called limestone. During the Miocene Period the land began to rise, for great changes were taking place all over the world. In the country we now call Egypt this limestone rock became dry land. Later by perhaps a dozen million years the Egyptians cut this rock into blocks and made their pyramids.

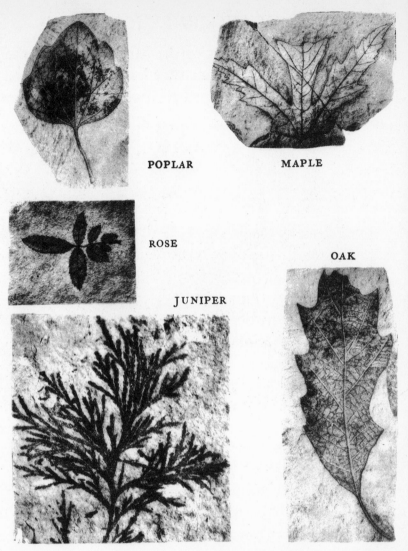

POPLAR   MAPLE

ROSE

OAK

JUNIPER

LEAVES OF THE MIOCENE PERIOD

Figure 156. These leaves grew in the states of Colorado and Washington during the Miocene Period. From *Plants of the Past* by F. H. Knowlton of U. S. Geological Survey.

RISE OF MIOCENE MOUNTAINS

During the latter part of the Miocene Period the apparently peaceful relations that had existed so long between the surface of the earth and the interior seemed

SWITZERLAND IN THE MIOCENE PERIOD

Figure 157. When you see the high Alps and many glaciers it is hard to believe that Switzerland once looked like this picture. Once a shallow sea and tropical forest covered this land. It was a weak place in the crust of the earth, so that wrinkles came and wore into jagged points and gave us the Alps. After Heer. From *Plants of the Past* by F. H. Knowlton of U. S. Geological Survey.

to have come to a close, for all over the world there were long stretches of land, weak places in the earth's crust, where wrinkles occurred. Worse even than that—the layers of rock actually folded and cracked. So recent was this upheaval that these scars remain to this day. There are huge snow-capped mountains and cracks in the earth where the surfaces are still slipping past each other and causing earthquakes. In some cases, as along the east coast of North America where the Appalachian Mountains are now, the land merely rose and did not wrinkle or fold.

The Mississippi River flowed into the Gulf of Mexico at a point not far from that at which the city of Vicksburg now stands. The map shows a slightly earlier epoch when the Gulf extended to the Ohio River. All the southern coast was under water as far north as Virginia. Florida was submerged. The West Indies had again emerged from the sea and except for the presence of a few volcanoes began to look much as they do today. North and South America were once more connected by a land bridge that was considerably wider than the present Isthmus of Panama, but active volcanoes made its use as a bridge precarious.

On the west coast the Gulf of California was larger than now and extended into territories we call California and Arizona. A remnant still existed of that strange land to the west of California. Oregon and Washington remained the scene of volcanic eruptions which covered hundreds of thousands of square miles with lava and ashes. We have already found that this disturbance extended to the land of the Yellowstone National Park and to Lake Florissant in Colorado.

CONTEST BETWEEN MOUNTAINS AND AIR

The coast of British Columbia and southern Alaska was very much as it is today, except that Bering Strait did not exist; for Asia and North America were connected by dry land. In the northeast, Greenland continued to be united to Canada, and the coast from New Jersey to Labrador extended farther eastward than now. The Gulf of St. Lawrence was smaller than now, and Hudson Bay did not exist.

There seems to be a constant struggle between the earth's crust and the air. The rock is ever wrinkling and folding and trying to erect lofty snow-capped mountains. The air, by its weapons of atoms and water and glaciers, is ever destroying these creations of the earth. The Greeks imagined such conflicts carried on by gods and goddesses called Titans. Javelins, lightning, and intrigue were used by them in geological conflicts. We have no Homer in modern geology to describe this conflict, greater than the siege of Troy. Perhaps Milton is our Homer, for he said:

"And Chaos, ancestor of Nature, hold
Eternal anarchy amidst the noise
Of endless wars, and by confusion stand:
For hot, cold, moist and dry, four champions fierce,
Strive here for mastery, and to battle bring
Their embryonic atoms.
. . . Chaos umpire sits,
By which he reigns; next him, high arbiter,
Chance governs all."

MIOCENE PERIOD

Far back in Devonian times there were mountains in the country we now call California and Oregon (Figure 50). They soon lost in the conflict and were worn down to a peneplain. At the end of the Permian the earth again thrust up its crags on the west coast of British Columbia, Oregon, Washington, and California (Figure 69). However, the atoms of O, water, and ice drove them back to well-rounded and wooded hills. Undaunted, in the Jurassic the earth wrinkled and created mountains in British Columbia and Idaho and made her first effort to raise the Sierra Nevada Mountains (Figure 108). But all in vain, for these peaks crumbled in millions of years as their predecessors had done. At the end of the Cretaceous Period the earth mustered her forces for a world-wide struggle and raised row on row of mountains where the Coast Range and Rocky Mountains are now (Figure 125). That air, "hot, cold, moist, and dry," always won, and during the long peaceful periods of the Eocene and Oligocene only low hills amid the forests and grassy plains were left to mark the earth's greatest efforts.

Now in the Miocene another conflict started, and the end of this struggle is not yet in sight. The earth wrinkled, cracked, and produced the Coast Range, the Sierra Nevada range, and the Rocky Mountains, with deep gulleys, valleys, and cliffs (Figure 158). As if to hurl defiance at the air, the earth threw out huge streams of lava from the cracks (Figure 159) formed by these upheavals. Upheavals they really were, for in California a

A MAP OF NORTH AMERICA IN THE MIOCENE PERIOD

Figure 158. In order to indicate the change in the outline of the continent a modern outline map has been printed over the Miocene land area. The outline map is published by Rand McNally and Company, by whose permission it is reproduced. The outline of the Miocene map is a modified copy of a drawing in *An Introduction to Historical Geology* by W.J. Miller, published by D. Van Nostrand Company.

great block of land hundreds of miles long tipped so that its eastern edge rose several thousand feet and its western edge sank into the land (Figure 160). It made the valley of California more prominent than before. This partly upturned block is called the Sierra Nevada Mountains.

Courtesy of the U. S. Geological Survey

A CRACK IN THE EARTH'S CRUST

Figure 159. This is a picture of a crack in the earth's surface at Chollowee Mountain, Tenn. The earth not only cracked but slipped, as shown by the displacement of the layers. Such a slip shakes the neighboring land and is called an earthquake. Photograph by the U. S. Geological Survey.

Those two great cracks where that giant block rose on its eastern edge and sank on its western edge are still there. That block, the size of a State, is still uneasy. On the eastern edge every now and then it rises a little and the Sierra Nevada Mountains are pushed higher in the air. On March 26, 1872, this block rose twenty feet where the eastern crack occurs. The shock "was felt from

Shasta to San Diego and points far beyond the border of Mexico. The tall trees of the Yosemite [valley] were waved about and bent like twigs, as the [earthquake] waves raced westward. Because of the sparse population, the casualties numbered fewer than 100, but the shock was probably much severer than the one that ruined so much of San Francisco in 1906. The air was charged with

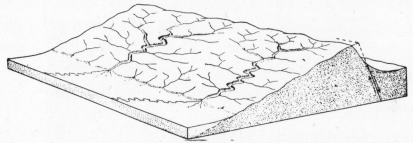

Courtesy of the American Museum of Natural History

HOW THE SIERRA NEVADA MOUNTAINS WERE MADE

Figure 160. This diagram illustrates the way in which that huge mass of the earth's crust was forced up like a block of river ice in a jam. The Yosemite Valley was carved deeper as the rainwater and later the glacier flowed down the sloping surface. From *The Story of the Yosemite Valley* by F. E. Matthes, published by the American Museum of Natural History.

dust for a whole day. Owens Lake was jostled into turbulence and long, high foaming waves. Water fountains reaching seventy-five feet in height were spurted from the writhing fissures and many massive landslides occurred." So writes R. A. Daly in *Our Mobile Earth*.

All these upheavals were spread over vast periods of time. If any man had lived during the titanic disturbances, he would have said that the mountains were as eternal as the plains; for the slight movements accompanied sometimes by earthquakes would have seemed to him trivial. Yet through the long ages, by these trivial changes, the mountains rose and fell. Perhaps the Sierra Nevadas are rising today about as fast as they ever did; yet we think of them as "everlasting hills." Perhaps as one earthquake shock after another adds a few feet to their height, some day they may be the loftiest mountains in the world. Then in the course of millions of years the air will win the conflict, and there will be low hills and grassy plains instead of the beautiful Sierra Nevadas with snow-capped peaks and great valleys like the Yosemite National Park.

All over the world in the Miocene the earth began to writhe, squirm, wrinkle, and fold. The Andes rose again, for since their last effort at the end of the Cretaceous Period, they had been sadly destroyed by the perpetual nibbling of erosion. Those quiet scenes in Switzerland (Figure 157) were slowly, very slowly destroyed, for the earth here wrinkled extensively. East and west wrinkles rose high in the air and then folded toward the north. Let us always remember, however, that the folding was ever so slow—probably no faster than the present rise of the Sierra Nevada Mountains; but after millions of years the effect was stupendous. Gullied by rain into innumerable valleys and torn by glaciers, the crumbling rock of these folds fell from their lofty heights. Now crags and broken peaks and terribly scarred mountains are all that is left of the magnificent folds that once rose against the air in serried ranks. One of the famous remnants is the Matterhorn (Figure 161). It is a portion of

Courtesy of Edward Arnold and Company

THE MATTERHORN SEEN FROM THE HÉRENS PASS

Figure 161. "A mighty mountain without roots, a stranger in a foreign land." A mere remnant of a great fold in the earth which was thrust up from the south. The wear and tear of ice, water, and air wore away those wrinkles and left the crags and peaks that we call the Alps. The rocks which make the Matterhorn came from folds which originally had lain 60 miles to the south. The dotted lines show the position of some of these folds. Photographed by J. Gaberell for *Structure of the Alps* by Leon W. Collet.

the front rank of a fold carried far north before the strength of the charge was exhausted.

–While the uneasy earth was squirming and wrinkling

under its blanket of air, no peace had settled down on
the animal kingdom. The tigers and dogs were becoming
stronger, and the horses were growing larger and faster.
It was a **grim** existence, in which most animals met with

Courtesy of Miss Alice B. Woodward

A MIOCENE SABER-TOOTH TIGER

Figure 162. No wonder the horse ran faster as time went on, when we see the
tiger Machaerodus growing ever stronger. From a drawing by Miss Alice
B. Woodward for *Evolution in the Past* by H. R. Knipe, published by
Herbert and Daniel, London.

a violent death. During the Miocene, Machaerodus (Figure 162) is a fair representative of the saber-tooth tiger,
the leader of the cat family. Although larger and swifter
than his ancestors, Hypohippus, the Miocene horse (Figure 163) all too often served as food for Machaerodus.

HYPOHIPPUS

Figure 163. A horse which lived in the forests of North America during the last part of the Miocene Period. After a drawing by C. R. Knight for *The Age of Mammals* by H. F. Osborn, published by Charles Scribner's Sons.

MIOCENE PERIOD

Now in the Miocene the historic rival of the cat family asserts himself. Descended from a savage creodont called Miacida, the wild dog is represented by *Daphoenodon superbus* (Figure 164), a powerful meat-eater, some-

Courtesy of W. B. Scott

DAPHOENODON SUPERBUS

Figure 164. Descended from Eocene creodonts called Miacidae, this small fox-like dog lived in North America during the early part of the Miocene Period. He is sometimes called a "bear-dog." Restored from a skeleton in the Carnegie Museum, Pittsburgh. From a *History of Land Mammals in the Western Hemisphere* by W. B. Scott of Princeton University, published by The Macmillan Company.

times called a "bear-dog," and destined to be perhaps the ancestor of man's best friend.

While tigers and bear-dogs were Hypohippus' major troubles, he also had some minor tormentors; horseflies

(Figure 165) and other flies (Figure 166) existed then as now. As if in contrast to the life of the rest of the fauna, the butterflies, apparently at peace with the world, hovered over the flowers on the shores of Lake Florissant much as they do now in Colorado. However, the insect world had its terrors then as now; for S. H. Scudder

Courtesy of the American Museum of Natural History

THERE WERE HORSE FLIES EVEN IN THE MIOCENE

Figure 165. That little horse Hypohippus had horse flies, *Tabanus parahippus*, for his minor troubles, just as his descendants have today. Of course his major trouble was the saber-tooth tiger. From "An Article About Colorado in the Miocene Period" by T. D. A. Cockerell of the University of Colorado, in *Natural History*, published by the American Museum of Natural History.

found in the fossils of Lake Florissant the dreaded tsetse fly (Figure 167) that now kills so many thousands of people in Africa by means of sleeping-sickness. It is particularly fatal to cattle and to many other large animals. So the horse had another deadly enemy, and it is possible, according to H. F. Osborn, that the tsetse fly may have caused the complete disappearance of many large mam-

[305]

mals that used to roam over the plains of North America. Perhaps these migrations of animals from Asia and Europe over those northern land bridges brought this deadly pest to America. Fortunately this fly is now found only in certain parts of Africa and southern Arabia. In America he perished as completely as did his victims, the camels, horses, and rhinoceroses that used to inhabit this land by the tens of thousands. We are not at all sure that the

FOSSIL FLY

Figure 166. A remarkably well-preserved fly of the Miocene Period. It was caught in the mud of Lake Florissant, Colorado. From a photograph of a specimen in the American Museum of Natural History.

mammals perished because of the fly, and as to tsetse himself, we have no idea why he became extinct, but we are very glad that he did.

How did our ancestors like this Miocene world? Did they grow stronger and more intelligent during these 12 million years? Were there any more family differences of opinion which caused groups of conservatives to go off by themselves and live ever afterward as their ancestors had done? Apparently the answer to these questions is that the primates flourished during the Miocene, grew larger, stronger, brighter, and learned more about walking on the ground. Perhaps during this period they

Courtesy of the U. S. National Museum

FOSSIL TSETSE FLY (GLOSSINA)

Figure 167. The tsetse fly causes sleeping-sickness in Africa and kills thousands of horses and cattle. Approximately 15 million years ago this fly lived in Colorado. Fortunately Colorado now has only harmless fossil tsetse flies. From *New Species of North American Fossil Beetles, Cockroaches, and Tsetse Flies* by T. D. A. Cockerell of the University of Colorado (Proceedings of the U. S. National Museum).

learned to defend themselves on the ground without always climbing that ancestral citadel, a tall tree. They traveled far and wide, for we find some of their jawbones and teeth in Spain, France, and India.

MIOCENE PERIOD

The change in climate had altered the dense forests of the Oligocene. Great plains of grass separated the tracts of woodlands. The primates that stayed in these temperate climates were forced to change their ways of living. The greater variety in their lives produced more brains, for those that were not bright enough to adapt themselves to new conditions perished. Being therefore unable to bring up a family of small primates, they fortunately were unable to perpetuate their stupidity. At this time, however, another group of primates reached their limit. They stayed by the trees, although they continued to spend a considerable part of their time on the ground. They may in millions of years have become so fixed in their habit of living partly in trees and partly on ground that they never could change. Then if, because of changed weather conditions, they could not find just the kind of home to which they were accustomed, they would probably die.

Those conservatives who could just reach the Miocene stage but could go no further we call great apes; they are living now in Africa, and there apparently they still find conditions much as they were back in the Miocene. They have now separated into several groups, but they all have a strong family resemblance, and probably they rather closely resemble our common ancestors. We have given the name Dryopithecus to this group of ancestors who lived in the Miocene of Asia, Europe, and Africa.

GORILLAS AND CHIMPANZEES

The gorillas (Figure 168) and the chimpanzees (Figure 169), now living in Africa, probably together give us a very good idea of the degree of intelligence of our

Courtesy of Mrs. May L. Jobe Akeley

GORILLA

Figure 168. A portrait bust by the late Carl Akeley of the American Museum of Natural History. It is said that it is an injustice to call our cousin ferocious. You see in this picture he looks thoughtful and not savage. (Copyright by Carl Akeley.)

great-grandfather Dryopithecus. The expression of his face and the way he walked is probably fairly well represented by the combination of gorilla and chimpanzee, for they are Miocene conservatives, although their ancestors had been progressives through all the interminable ages that preceded. They had reached their limit, these Miocene gorillas, and could go no further.

A GOOD LIKENESS OF OUR MIOCENE ANCESTOR

Figure 169. If our ancestor of the Miocene Period had had his photograph taken, it probably would not have differed much from this photograph of a chimpanzee which was taken by Herbert Lang on the American Museum expedition to the Belgian Congo.

Perhaps the gorilla was not willfully a conservative. It may be his family wandered into a country that suited them so well—so much like the combination of forest and plain in which they had been developed—that they had no cause to change their way of living. So naturally they kept on being gorillas. Why should they do otherwise, so long as the forests, the plains, and the weather remained so satisfactory for gorilla welfare? After millions of years of this contented life the gorilla could not have changed if he had wanted to, because he had become fixed in his habits—a "living fossil." If conditions in Africa changed, if the forests disappeared and the weather grew colder, the gorillas and chimpanzees would probably perish, for, being now "living fossils," they have lost the ability to change. We do not mean that they have become mentally stupider than they were in the Miocene days of their ancestor Dryopithecus. We merely mean that now there is a great sameness among gorillas. Little gorillas, if they went to school, would be nearly all equally bright. In the football games in such a school there would not be much difference between the players. It would be almost a matter of indifference whether the coach put John Gorilla into the game as a "quarter-back" or as a "center." Of course even here there would be some choice, in which a gorilla coach could show his skill. However, almost any eleven of young gorilla students would make a good team; but the same is not true, as we well know, among the white primates. It is this uniformity in the gorilla's ability that would prevent him from surviving a great catastrophe like a glacial epoch.

When a race of animals has a considerable variation among its individuals—when brothers are not just alike and some prefer hot weather and others cold weather, when some are good musicians and others are good football players—then when earthquakes come and the weather changes, some will be sure to survive. Those that survive will have children much like themselves who can live under the new conditions. Thus that race of animals will change, sometimes in appearance, sometimes in ability. This change is not always for the better. It does not always mean that such a race of animals is going to be brighter than its ancestors. In some cases very much the opposite has taken place. You remember that some mammals which ran through the forest on four feet became whales and probably grew stupider instead of brighter; at any rate they failed to stay with the progressive branches of the mammals such as tigers, primates, and dogs.

Why are the children of one group of animals so much alike that we call that group "living fossils," and why are there such differences in the ability and even in the appearance of children of another group? We do not know. Perhaps the homes of the conservative animals are satisfactory and stay satisfactory. Perhaps the homes of the progressive families of animals are not satisfactory, and more than that, perhaps such homes are always changing, so that small differences among the children become very advantageous; for they may enable some children to survive and prosper under new conditions, when other children who were a little different would suffer. However, we do not know. Some day you will probably read of new discoveries in this interesting subject.

WHEN DID DRYOPITHECUS LIVE?

There is another problem that is not yet solved: from time to time you will probably read of the progress that is being made, and perhaps some of you may assist in finding the answer. The question is: Did Dryopithecus, the common ancestor of man **and** the great apes, live first

Dryopithecus' diary would be highly valued now-a-days.

in the early Pliocene, about 5 million years ago, or did he live in the Oligocene, about 30 million years back? While waiting for an answer to these questions we assume that Dryopithecus lived during the latter part of the Miocene Period. Some think those great apes, the gorillas and chimpanzees, separated from the family of the progressive primates as far back as the Eocene, or about 50 million years ago. This problem is of great human interest, for it seriously affects our family history. Therefore it will be interesting and almost exciting in the years to come to read the various biographies of Dryopithecus.

Do not think that life in the Miocene consisted only of the animals we have mentioned; there were many, many more, such as rhinoceroses, venomous snakes, deer, and bison. Our space is limited, however, so that we must write no more about this interesting 12 million years of the "Less Recent."

XVIII. PLIOCENE PERIOD

THE Pliocene Period—meaning "More Recent"—began 7 million years ago and lasted 6 million years. It was a time of rising of lands, increasing cold, and the migration of huge mammals called mastodons. The most intelligent, ingenious, and destructive of all mammals emerged in this period as the leader of the primates; we call him Man. As if to anticipate their bondage and future slaughter, many of the larger mammals became extinct in North America, either at the close of this period or at the beginning of the next.

After our long journey and intimate contact with the magnificent creations of the animal kingdom, we feel sad as we reach that time when the modern era first begins to take shape. As we look about us we see our fellow men exterminating the animal kingdom at an incredible and needless rate. Not many generations from now and certainly in our present geological period, only those large animals will be left which are kept in reservations or carefully bred for man's use. Evolution in the animal kingdom will have ceased except as man will have directed its

[315]

course by the careful selection of those whose special characteristics he wishes to retain.

During the 6 million years of the "More Recent," the land of North America rose to a considerable extent, so that the continent began to look very much like the maps in geography books (Figure 170). Greenland, toward the end of the period, became entirely separated from Canada. The depression that allowed the water to flow between these great bodies of land and to connect the Arctic Ocean with the Atlantic, did not extend to the east coast of North America; for then, as for several periods in the past, the coast line extended far out to sea, in some cases for 100 miles. Those historic rivers, the St. Lawrence, Hudson, Delaware, and James, still joined the Atlantic Ocean far to the east where now fishes swim in several hundred feet of water.

Florida had ceased to be an island and looked very much like a peninsula, but it did not extend so far south as at present. The West Indies, on the other hand, were almost modern in appearance, at least so far as their outline was concerned. North and South America were still united, but the land bridge was not so wide as in the Miocene. Those volcanoes that must have terrified the migrating animals were still there. In fact a zone of active volcanoes extended all up the Pacific coast as far as the southern part of British Columbia. Then they appeared again in Alaska, where they are found to this day.

The Mississippi River still flowed into the Gulf of

MAP OF NORTH AMERICA IN THE PLIOCENE PERIOD

Figure 170. In most places the land extended beyond the present coast line as is shown by the outline map of North America by Rand McNally and Company. This present-day outline map has been printed over the Pliocene land areas. From *Historical Geology* by Charles Schuchert of Yale University, published by John Wiley and Sons, Inc.

Mexico at a point not far from the modern city of Vicksburg. It had to begin to cut a channel again, for the whole valley rose several hundred feet during this period.

The Pacific coast began to look much as it does now except that the coast line was in most cases farther to the west than at present. The Rocky Mountains continued to rise and at the end of this period reached nearly their present height. That partly upturned block that began to raise its eastern edge high in the air in the Miocene continued to tip and to rise even more in this period. The rainwater, as it drained off over the western slope of this unsettled block, cut deep gullies that became large V-shaped valleys with steep sides. In the next period the cold became so intense that glaciers were formed, and these V-shaped valleys were gouged and scraped into U-shaped valleys. This upturned block of land, as big as a State, and these deep rain-washed valleys turning to U-shaped valleys made some of the grandest scenery in the world. Yosemite National Park is one of these valleys (Figure 66).

You have probably heard of the Great American Desert which lies east of the Sierra Nevada Mountains and between them and the Rocky Mountains. This stretch of desolation was caused by that upturned block of land, the Sierra Nevada Mountains. The wind in that part of the country usually blows from the west. On its way over the Pacific Ocean it has picked up many of those little globules of water which we have described in connection with glaciers. When this wind tries to climb over the tops of the Sierra Nevada Mountains it loses them, for when air rises to the top of a mountain it becomes cold. Then it cannot hold so many globules of water and they fall as snowflakes or raindrops. Consequently when the air has passed over the mountains and started on its journey east it is nearly dry and can give scarcely any rain. Such a condition always causes a desert, and a desert we have to the east of the Sierra Nevada Mountains even to this day. Also that desert will be there until the mountains are again worn down to a peneplain and once more the moist air from off the Pacific can blow over the low wooded hills and bring rain to the thirsty country. As they have done in some other deserts, men some day may bring water in canals and pipes from distant mountains and thus defy the Sierra Nevadas.

This new rise of the Rocky Mountains and the Sierra Nevadas also raised the land between them by several thousand feet. The Colorado River began at once to cut a new and deeper channel as it flowed over its ancient course on this plateau. It has been undermining its banks and carrying the debris downstream for several million years and now has cut a canyon a mile deep—the most wonderful canyon in the world (Figure 171).

Far back in the Eocene there developed a family of little elephants that must have had ancestors among the archaic mammals of the Cretaceous Period and perhaps even earlier. The oldest member of this family that has

Courtesy of the Union Pacific Railroad

THE GRAND CANYON OF THE COLORADO RIVER

Figure 171. For several million years the Colorado River has been cutting this deep channel in the solid rock. If the land does not rise again, the river will some day wear away all the rock that is shown in this picture. Then there will be stretches of plains and low well-rounded hills covered with grass and forests. Such will be Colorado millions of years from now. View from Toroweap Point—a high pinnacle on the north rim

ever been found lived in Egypt on the banks of the primitive Nile, sometimes called the Ur-Nile. This elephant's name is Moeritherium (Figure 172). He was only two feet high and was fond of bathing.

The members of that elephant family were as marvelous in some respects as their successors, the Egyptian pri-

Courtesy of the American Museum of Natural History

MOERITHERIUM, A PRIMITIVE ELEPHANT

Figure 172. Discovered by the British geologist, C. W. Andrews, this small elephant was only 2 feet tall. He lived part of the time in the water and is the most ancient elephant so far discovered. He may have lived as far back as the Eocene. After a drawing by C. R. Knight under the direction of H. F. Osborn at the American Museum of Natural History. From *Mastodons and Mammoths of North America* by H. F. Osborn, published by the American·Museum of Natural History.

mates who carved the Sphinx. Unlike the Egyptians, the elephants were pioneers and explorers. They traveled far and wide wherever they could walk. Of the sixteen different groups of elephants that originated in Egypt or perhaps in some cases in India, eleven reached America (Figure 173). "An insatiable wanderlust," says H. F. Osborn, "has always possessed the souls of elephants as it has those of the tribes and races of man. Not only to overcome the changes and chances of this mortal life, but also to gratify their intelligent curiosity ever to explore fresh forests, pastures, fields, rivers and streams they

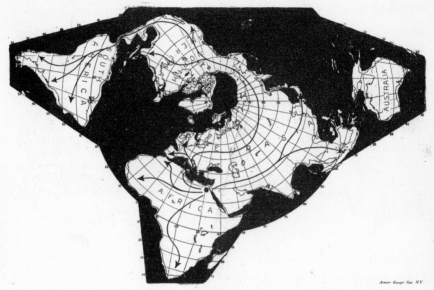

Amer Geogr Soc N.Y.

Courtesy of the American Geographical Society

MAP OF THE ROUTES FOLLOWED BY ELEPHANTS

Figure 173. Starting in Egypt these dignified pioneers traveled the thousands of miles to South America. They could not get to Australia because they had no boats. From *Mastodons and Mammoths of North America* by H. F. Osborn, published by the American Museum of Natural History.

have gone to the very ends of the earth and have far surpassed man in adapting their clothing and teeth to all possible conditions of life. Thus the romances of elephant migration and conquest are second only to the romances of human migration and conquest."

[322]

MASTODONS

Several of the groups of elephants were so much alike that we call them all mastodons. The earliest mastodon which has left us his skeleton was Phiomia (Figure 174). He lived in Egypt in the Oligocene Period, and his descendants, as they carried out the traditions of this

Copyright by the American Museum of Natural History

PHIOMIA, THE FOUNDER OF THE LONG-JAWED FAMILY

Figure 174. Way back in the Oligocene of Egypt the descendants of Phiomia inherited her long jaws. As time went on and the family traveled far, they grew larger and the family characteristic grew more pronounced. Restorations by Osborn and Knight at the American Museum of Natural History. H. F. Osborn was the discoverer of Phiomia. From *Mastodons and Mammoths of North America* by H. F. Osborn.

Viking family, grew larger and traveled farther. Their jaws, always long, became longer. Finally in the Pliocene Period these elephants reached South Dakota (Figure 175). They had traveled by way of Siberia and Alaska and had spent several million years on the journey. Then there were mastodons famous for their peculiar teeth ("serrate-toothed," Figure 176). Apparently,

[323]

THE LONG-JAWED FAMILY, TRILOPHODON GIGANTEUS

Figure 175. These are the descendants of little Phiomia. That lower jaw served them well, for they were among the largest mammals of their time. This is a picture of the way they lived in South Dakota in the Pliocene. It took the family the entire Miocene Period of 12 million years to travel from Egypt to South Dakota. After a painting by C. R. Knight made under the direction of H. F. Osborn for the American Museum of Natural History. From

A SERRATE-TOOTHED MASTODON

Figure 176. This fellow died in Texas in the Pliocene. He was about 6 feet high and was fond of leaves. His family left home in the Miocene Period and traveled by way of Gobi, where one of his relatives died and left a jawbone for the expedition of the American Museum of Natural History. After a painting by C. R. Knight, made under the direction of H. F. Osborn. From *Mastodons and Mammoths of North America* by H. F. Osborn.

like European white primates, a large number tried to come to Canada and America, and many of them succeeded.

The old contest between the horse and the tiger continued during this period. The horses grew large, swift, and numerous. Hipparion is the name of the leading horse of the Pliocene (Figure 177). At last he had a hoof as any self-respecting horse should have. It took him 50 million years to lose those four useless toes and develop a hoof. Therefore we must not be surprised if we find that we humans have changed little since the time of the Greeks or even the Egyptians; what are a few thousand years compared with the 50 million years required by the horse to lose four toes?

During this period the saber-tooth tiger apparently reached its maximum size (Figure 178). Early in the next period these wonderful creatures died; they left no descendants. They had been 50 million years developing from the savage meat-eating creodonts. Then they suddenly vanished, for reasons unknown. About the same time the vast herds of horses and the innumerable camels and rhinoceroses became nearly extinct so far as North America was concerned. Apparently some camels, at least, survived through the Pleistocene Period, according to a discovery recently made in Utah and described by A. S. Romer of the University of Chicago in *Science* of June 6, 1928. Other animals came to take their places, such as the bear, royal bison, and the *Mastodon americanus.*

PLIOCENE HORSES

.Figure 177.

"For over grassy plain, and vale, and hill,
 Wide rove the creatures at their own sweet will;
Free as the air their opening nostrils draw,
Wild as the waves that toss their spray to shore.
Changed times indeed their progeny will see,
As to his will man bends their energy;
And varied be the parts they will sustain,
In bondage held, controlled by bit and rein;—
To run the measured course at headlong pace;
And tear along in maddening chariot race;
To bear the knight, with spear and blazoned shield,
Or in joust, or on the battlefield;
To mount the hunter as he hawking goes;
To chase the fox and troll in circus shows;
And harnessed be, alert and at Man's command,
Or on the road or on the furrowed land.
Ready in war, and toil and sport and play,
As Man appoints to listen and obey.
 But here, wild hearts, no bit is yours to fret,
 Nor toil to know; your master tarries yet."

From *Nebula to Man* by **H. R. Knipe.**

MACHAERODUS, THE PLIOCENE SABER-TOOTH TIGER

Figure 178. Did bigger and faster horses force the tiger to be large or to be hungry? Did the bigger tiger make the horse grow larger and run faster or be eaten? However you answer these questions, the result was a magnificent tiger and a wonderful horse. From *Nebula to Man* by H. R. Knipe.

Courtesy of J. M. Dent and Sons, Ltd.

Smilodon (Figure 188) and Machaerodus had spent so many million years in reaching tiger perfection that we cannot help a feeling of regret at their untimely death. If they had lived one period longer, our immediate ancestors would have had the pleasure of meeting them.

Over in Asia there were developed at this time some mammals that some day, when kept as slaves by man, were destined to prove as useful as the horse. They were the cattle. Those that man has domesticated never migrated over the land bridge of Siberia and Alaska as did the mastodons and some of the early mammals. They were brought to North America in boats from Europe only when the European white primates made the last great mammal migration to America.

We have reserved till the last in this chapter the most important animals of all, the primates. With the increasingly cold weather, the forests slowly lost their tropical appearance. Those progressive primates that did not migrate to warmer lands had to be constantly changing their mode of living. Of course, as usual, the change was made by the relentless law of the elimination of the unfit. During this period they evidently learned not only to defend themselves on the ground but to use tools of some crude kind; and late in the period, it is thought by some, they used sharp-pointed and sharp-edged stones as scrapers for the preparation of the furs that they may have used for added warmth; for during the final part of this period they may have protected themselves from cold by the use of skins of other animals. Such progressive primates we call men and women, or human beings.

This is another subject on which there is a wide difference of opinion. When did our ancestors begin to use sharp-pointed stones and stone scrapers? J. Reid Moir in England has discovered a great many pieces of flint of this period that he thinks were made by those progressive primates or early men, and a number of distinguished geologists agree with him. Some of these flints are kept in the British Museum. Yet it is not certain that they were chipped by man. They may have been broken by ordinary wear and tear of the weather and by the pressure of rocks. From time to time you will probably learn about new investigations, and some day you may know just when your ancestors were bright enough to chip stones into sharp points for use as tools.

In 1903 Dr. Dubois of Holland discovered in Java most of the skull, some of the teeth, and one bone of a Pliocene primate. By comparing these bones with those of other primates and with the skeletons of other very early men, it has been possible to draw a fair picture of this contemporary of our Pliocene ancestors. His name is Pithecanthropus (Figure 179), and his portrait should be hung in our dining-room.

W. D. Matthew, professor of palaeontology in the University of California, has published in *Natural His-*

tory (Vol. XXVIII) a very interesting story of a group of such ape-men as Pithecanthropus: "Three ape-men come trotting down one of the trails, tall, upright, broad-

Courtesy of the American Museum of Natural History

PITHECANTHROPUS

Figure 179. A contemporary of our ancestors of 1 or 2 million years back. This particular gentleman lived in Java until a few years ago, when he moved to Holland and took up his residence in a safety deposit box. He didn't have to hire a large box, for he had a careless way of losing his bones. When he left Java he had only a skull, one bone, and a few teeth—at least that is all his friends could find when they arranged for his passage. After a model by J. H. McGregor at the American Museum of Natural History.

shouldered, their gleaming brown skin half concealed by sparse black hair. They run at an easy jog-trot, steady, watchful, with quick, flashing glances to right and left, noting the least sound or movement in the forest, a

[331]

PITHECANTHROPUS WHEN HE WAS A YOUNG MAN IN JAVA

Figure 180. Drawn by A. A. Jansson for *The Ape Man in Java* by **W. D.** Matthew of the University of California (*Natural History*, Vol. XXVIII.

broken leaf by the trail, a displaced branch underfoot.

"Every now and then they slow down to a walk or stop to examine some new or unusual object, track, or mark, crowding around it to see better, pointing and gesturing and expressing ideas in a sort of rude language of clicks and grunts. In their manner, their activity, and quick, changing interest, they are like a group of small boys perhaps on their way to the swimming pool (Figure 181) at the back of the woodlot. But they are tall, six feet in height, powerfully proportioned, with heavy muscular torso and limbs of maturity, and the black hair over body, arms and legs, while scanty for a beast, is too heavy to seem quite human. . . . None of the jungle beasts is safe from the ape-men's restless curiosity and deviltries.

"A movement and rustle in a leafy covert brings a shower of heavy and well-directed stones, which serves to dislodge a tiger lurking there. He springs for the moment into the open, then slinks off, bruised and battered, well aware that he stands but little chance of coming to close quarters with these active, wily enemies, who at last resort could always scramble up a tree out of reach and thence continue the attack with sticks and branches. The tiger driven off, the ape-men amuse themselves by pestering some of the smaller animals, routing out some of them from their holes or sheltered corners around the roots of trees, and exchanging missiles and abuse with a troop of monkeys in the tree-tops. . . .

"Does this rude sketch sound like the escapades of a gang of bad little boys? I hope so. Because that is just what the ape-men were, as I think of them. Clever and restless, mischievous, inconsequent, irresponsible, some-

Courtesy of the American Museum of Natural History

"TEASING THE GIANT TORTOISE"

Figure 181. "Like a gang of bad little boys, the ape-men topple the huge reptile over the bank to the sandy margin of the pool, where he lies helpless and snapping furiously at the sticks with which his tormentors prod him." Drawn by A. A. Jansson for *The Ape Man of Java* by W. D. Matthew of the University of California (*Natural History*, Vol. XXVIII.)

how I can't help liking them in spite of their naughtiness. And with the spirit of the gamin was combined the strength and hardiness and independence of the grown man, the savage and bestial face of the great apes, but the body and limbs of quite human type, only clothed with more or less of a coat of hair. A singular combination, based, as we shall see, upon very scanty evidence, yet I think on the whole the most probable concept that we can build up from such facts as are to be had. Some day, when Java or other regions of central and southern Asia have been more extensively explored for fossils, we shall know how near this picture is to fact."

Another group of pioneer primates traveled to the land we now call England. A skull of one of these early men has been found imbedded in the soil that was accumulated during the Pliocene Period at Piltdown. It is therefore spoken of as the Piltdown skull. This man, Eoanthropus or "dawn-man" (Figure 182), perhaps chipped pieces of flint into sharp-pointed stones with which he may have prepared the skins he used for clothing. He wasn't very bright, but he was one of the brightest animals of that time, for he probably knew that a sharp stone was better for some purposes than a round stone. "His history is shrouded in darkness"; where he came from is unknown. Perhaps he had become a "living fossil" and was displaced by another wave of more progressive primates.

With the close of this period comes the end of the successive supremacies of the great fishes, reptiles, and four-footed mammals. In the next chapter we shall find the irresistible power of the progressive primates already asserting itself. These primates in the next period will de-

Courtesy of the American Museum of Natural History

EOANTHROPUS OF PILTDOWN, ENGLAND

Figure 182. The first Briton we know of. He left a part of his skull to tell us that he was there. After a model by J. H. McGregor of the American Museum of Natural History.

velop to such an extent that they will understand a large part of the law of evolution. Then they will use it as a tool for their own advantage. As ruthlessly as *Tyrannosaurus rex* or Smilodon, they will eliminate all animals, fish, flesh, or fowl, that oppose their progress. From their knowledge of evolution they will carefully select the

[336]

parents, that the offspring may suit man's convenience. Thus they will raise hens that will lay an incredible number of eggs, and horses with a speed greater than that imparted by a fear of Smilodon.

XIX. PLEISTOCENE PERIOD

WE COME now to the last period in the earth's history. It is called Pleistocene, meaning "Most Recent," and is the shortest of all the periods; it started about 1 million years ago. So far as we are concerned it is the most eventful epoch in the history of the earth. During this brief and stormy time the primates whom we call men and women developed very rapidly. From being barely able to stand erect, use a wooden club, and perhaps make crude flint tools, they became men who dressed themselves in skins and were able to paint on the walls of caves colored pictures which are the admiration of artists even today.

The period is also known as the Ice Age. Great glaciers came and went during this million years. In America, the last glacier disappeared from the region of New York City about 38,000 years ago and in Europe from the southern part of Sweden about 12,000 years ago. Parts of the great glaciers are still found in Greenland, the northeastern part of North America, and the Antarctic continent. Until we can roam through a forest-covered Greenland on our summer vacations we cannot claim that the Ice Age is entirely past; for you remember that during nearly all the 1,000 million years of the earth's history, Greenland has been a warm country with thick forests. To have Greenland covered with a huge glacier is unusual from a geological point of view, and, geologically speaking, is probably a temporary condition.

Those mysterious glaciers began to form in Canada and Greenland at the beginning of the Pleistocene Period. After thousands of years the ice spread far and wide and began to cover the northern States. The wind took tens of thousands of years to evaporate from the ocean enough little globules of the water which, when turned into snowflakes and then into ice, made this giant glacier. And giant it really was, for in some places in Canada it may have been 10,000 feet thick—two miles of solid ice.

Then Canada became warmer; the globules of water fell as rain instead of snow. Slowly, very slowly, the ice melted and disappeared. Four and perhaps five times the ice came and went, and each invasion and withdrawal took an interminable time; altogether more than a million years of the earth's history are involved in these mighty pulsations.

These glaciers were destructive phenomena, more destructive than any of the fauna, even than *Tyrannosaurus rex* or Carcharodon. They withered the forests by their blighting cold and then tore up the ground and piled it high in the form of hills of gravel. They changed the courses of rivers, and when they melted and withdrew, left lakes where before there had been dry land.

When the glacier reached its farthest south in North America a large part of the country now called Canada and the United States was under ice (Figure 183). Each time the glacier came south it stayed as an unwelcome visitor for tens of thousands of years and held as prisoners all those vast clouds of water globules which made its ice.

If the progressive primates had published geographies in Europe at this time, they would have drawn some very queer maps. The receding water had exposed the ocean bottom for hundreds of miles from the present coast line. Figure 184 shows how the map of Europe looked in those days. A broad belt of land extended from the countries we call France and Germany northwest to Greenland. That famous river, the Rhine, flowed north into the Arctic Ocean, and the Thames was probably a branch of the Rhine. The Seine River flowed into a deep gorge which we speak of as the English Channel River. This river flowed through a valley or canyon whose sides rose hundreds of feet. These rivers tumbled into the Atlantic Ocean through gorges that were much like the Colorado canyon of today, only on a smaller scale. There must have been wild scenery in those glacial days.

At the Straits of Gibraltar the water was shallow. When the ocean's level was lowered because of the stealing of water by the glaciers, this land was exposed and became a land bridge that connected Europe and Africa.

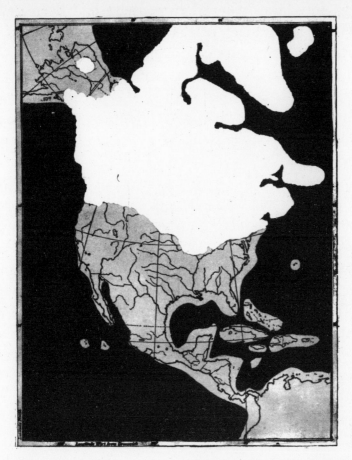

A MAP OF NORTH AMERICA IN THE PLEISTOCENE PERIOD

Figure 183. The white area indicates the land which at one time or another was covered with ice during the Pleistocene Period. The modern outline map clearly shows the greater land area in this period. (Outline map, published by Rand McNally and Company, by whose permission it is reproduced.) The contours of the continent and ice area were derived from a drawing in *Geology* by Chamberlin and Salisbury, published by Henry Holt and Company.

Then a curious thing happened to the Mediterranean Sea, for it began to dry up. In the Mediterranean today, the water evaporates faster than it can be supplied by

Courtesy of John Bartholomew and Son, Ltd.

MAP OF EUROPE DURING INTERGLACIAL TIMES

Figure 184. The Mediterranean Sea consisted of two large lakes separated by a land bridge that connected Italy with Sicily and with Africa. Greece was united with Asia Minor. From *Antiquity of Man in Europe* by James Geikie.

such rivers as the Danube, Nile, and Rhone. If it were not for the connection with the Atlantic Ocean at Gibraltar it would evaporate so rapidly that it would become a series of large lakes instead of an inland sea. This is just what happened in the glacial epoch. There was a land bridge connecting Italy, Sicily, and Africa and another that connected Greece with Asia Minor.

Of course all this new land was not due to the stealing of the water from the ocean by the glaciers. A great deal of this change in the map was caused by the rise of the land.

Like an irresistible horde of conquering globules which had massed together in giant blocks of ice, the European glaciers devastated the land almost as extensively and quite as slowly as did the American glaciers. Growing larger and larger in Norway and Sweden, they extended as far as London and covered all Denmark and part of northern Germany. At the same time another great ice-sheet spread from the Alps and covered all of the country we now call Switzerland and parts of Germany, France, Austria, and Italy. Nearly all the island of Corsica was under a glacier. As in North America, these European glaciers appeared and disappeared four times during the Pleistocene Period. Figure 185 is a map of the extent of this European glacier during its fourth and last appearance. Many other parts of the world were frozen by these masses of ice during the "Most Recent."

Thick furs were very fashionable garments for the fauna in the Pleistocene days. Herds of reindeer and huge woolly mammoths crossed the frozen rivers of France when the ice-sheets were descending from the

Alps. In North America, the *Mastodon americanus* (Figure 186) wandered over the land in herds of several hun-

Courtesy of John Bartholomew and Son, Ltd.

MAP OF EUROPE DURING THE FOURTH GLACIAL EPOCH

Figure 185. The white areas represent the part of the continent covered by the glaciers. From *Antiquity of Man in Europe* by James Geikie.

dreds as the modern buffalo used to do on our western plains.

Another animal which is not dressed for warm weather is the musk ox (Figure 187). Now he is found only on the shores of the Arctic Ocean. In the Pleistocene, how-

AMERICAN MASTODONS

Figure 186. "Fossil remains of this animal are found throughout the eastern and central states. Many specimens have been discovered in draining swamp-lands about Chicago." From a painting in Ernest R. Graham Hall by C. R. Knight.

ever, he ate moss and grass in New Jersey and Kentucky. Our old friend the saber-tooth tiger disappeared during this period. Smilodon and Machaerodus were the last leaders of this powerful branch of the cat family.

Courtesy of the New York Zoölogical Society

MUSK OX

Figure 187. A very thick fur protects him from the cold of the Arctic Circle where he now lives, although in the Pleistocene Period he roamed over Virginia and Kentucky. After a photograph by E. R. Sanborn, New York Zoölogical Society.

(Figure 188). The peace-loving American horse (Figure 189) disappeared with the tiger, and many of them doubtless disappeared into the tiger.

Near the present city of Los Angeles there was in this period a "tar-pool" which acted as a cruel trap for all these animals. If an animal ventured too far on its surface in search of food, he invariably got caught and slowly sank into the tar. It was as dangerous as the quicksands in some of our ponds and on an occasional beach.

Courtesy of the American Museum of Natural History.

SMILODON, THE SABER-TOOTH TIGER

Figure 188. This tiger lived in North and South America during the first part of the Pleistocene Period. Fortunately for us, he no longer roams through the forests. After a drawing by C. R. Knight of the American Museum of Natural History.

The more the victims struggled, the deeper they sank. Their cries must have echoed through the forest, for other animals came not to help but to devour them. Then these last comers in their turn became entangled in the pool (Figure 190). Thousands of bones have been dug from this spot and are now in the museum in Los Angeles.

PLEISTOCENE PERIOD

Perhaps it was during the long warm times between those four great ice periods that the Imperial Mammoth lived in Nebraska and Texas (Figure 191), for he ap-

Courtesy of W. B. Scott

A PLEISTOCENE HORSE IN TEXAS

Figure 189. Equus Scotti is his name. He was the last of his race, until the Spaniards brought his cousins from Europe to Texas. From *History of Land Mammals in the Western Hemisphere* by W. B. Scott of Princeton University, published by The Macmillan Company.

parently did not have such a warm fur coat as *Mastodon americanus*. He was a majestic creature and looks as if he were proud of the great plains over which his rule was supreme.

When the ice melted, retreated to the north, and finally disappeared from nearly all of the continent of North America, great changes would have been necessary in maps if any had been printed in those days. A sheet of ice covering several million square miles, and from one to two miles thick, has enormous weight. It would crush almost anything, and the earth's crust actually did bend under the load. The coasts of Labrador, Nova Scotia, and Maine were pushed far under the water, although the level of the ocean was lower, as we have seen, than it

Courtesy of the Los Angeles Museum

THE TAR POOL

Figure 190. Southern California in the Pleistocene Period. From a painting by C. R. Knight at the Los Angeles Museum.

used to be. New beaches were cut by the waves. Then after the ice had gone and the land rose again, these beaches were raised, and now you find them hundreds of feet above the sea, which again is busy cutting new beaches at its present level.

Because the land was pushed down by the weight of the ice, the water from the melting glacier sometimes formed pools where the land was depressed. As the ice melted, these pools overflowed and became the source of some of our largest rivers. The more the ice melted and

[349]

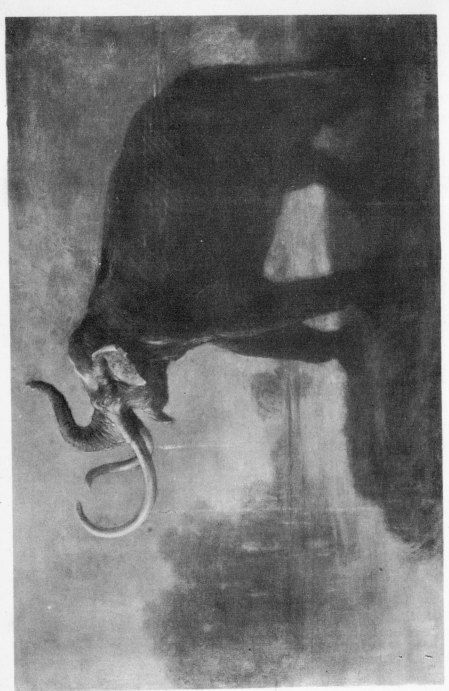

IMPERIAL MAMMOTH OF NEBRASKA AND TEXAS

Figure 191. After a painting by C. R. Knight in the American Museum of Natural History. From *Mastodons and*

the ice-sheet retreated north, the larger some of these pools grew. Finally they became our Great Lakes. The maps in Figures 192, 193, and 194 show the successive

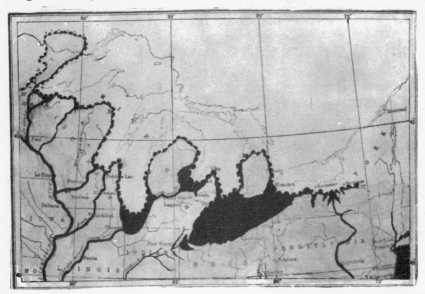

Courtesy of the Smithsonian Institution

RETREAT OF THE ICE SHEET AND FORMATION OF GREAT LAKES

Figure 192. Those great pools of water at the edge of the melting glacier overflowed through Finger Lakes and past the place where Harrisburg, Pa., now stands. Another overflow channel was near the present drainage canal at Chicago. Also these lakes flowed into Rock River, Portage River, and St. Croix River. From *History of the Great Lakes* by F. B. Taylor, Annual Report of Smithsonian Institution, 1912.

stages in the retreat of the glacier and the formation of the Great Lakes.

After the ice melted, the land rose very slowly to nearly its former height, but it has never returned entirely to its first position; perhaps some day it will. At

[351]

one time, just as the ice had melted and the land was still considerably depressed where the ice had been, the Atlantic Ocean flowed in to take the place of the melting

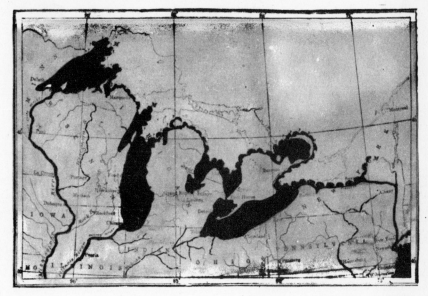

RETREAT OF ICE SHEET AND FORMATION OF GREAT LAKES

Figure 193. From time to time the ice-water in these great pools overflowed and made new channels to the Atlantic Ocean. This map shows the beginning of the Mohawk-Syracuse outlet and the Port Huron outlet. As before, we have the Chicago and St. Croix outlets, through which some water flowed into the Mississippi River and then to the Gulf of Mexico. From *History of the Great Lakes* by F. B. Taylor, Annual Report of Smithsonian Institution, 1912.

glacier. The ocean flowed up the Gulf of St. Lawrence as far as that great ice pool that we call Lake Ontario. It flowed south over the country now occupied by Lake Champlain and the Hudson River valley, so that New

WHALES IN LAKE CHAMPLAIN

England was an island. Whales must have circumnavigated this island, for one of them became stranded and left his skeleton on a beach of Lake Champlain.

Courtesy of the Smithsonian Institution

RETREAT OF ICE SHEET AND THE FORMATION OF THE GREAT LAKES

Figure 194. The ice sheet at this stage has retreated so far that the map looks almost like the one in our geographies. There is one queer outlet at North Bay through the Ottawa River that does not exist today. From *History of the Great Lakes* by F. B. Taylor, Annual Report of the Smithsonian Institution, 1912.

Like a rubber ball that has been dented, the crust of the earth gradually recovered from the terrific weight of the glacier. Then as the land rose the old beaches rose with it, and New England was no longer an island. We are not surprised then to learn that the whale's skeleton was found on one of these raised beaches several hundred feet above the present surface of Lake Champlain.

As our story comes to a close, let us study our own family history and learn, if we can, when and where our immediate ancestors, the European white primates, first appear. We have followed the development of the primates from a small tree-living animal, which lived 50 to 100 million years ago, to the ape type of animal that walked on his hind legs and perhaps in the late Pliocene Period chipped pieces of flint which he probably used as tools to assist him in preparing skins for his protection against the cold.

When a primate becomes sufficiently intelligent to use sticks and crudely worked stones as tools or weapons, we call him a man. There is no sharp distinction between a man primate and an ape primate. The one is evolved as gradually from the other as the hoofed horse was evolved from the five-toed horse.

Life during the million years of the Pleistocene became very strenuous for the primates in the northern hemisphere. The encroachment of the grassy plains on the forests caused many migrations among our forest-loving ancestors. Also those great pulsations of advancing and retreating ice-sheets forced the primates either to move to other climates or rather radically to change their mode of living. Probably both these things happened. The great territories, Europe, Africa, and North America, that were connected with Central Asia by land bridges, were time after time invaded by primates. As a general rule each succeeding invasion consisted of more intelligent and better-developed primates than the preceding; yet that was not always the case.

The first European of the Pleistocene who was kind enough to leave his bones for our museums lived in Germany near the place now made famous by the great University of Heidelberg, and he is known as the Heidelberg Man. In those days Europe was warm, for the first glacier had come and gone. Europe probably enjoyed a climate milder than at present. The Heidelberg Man or his ancestors had wandered far in the search for food. Perhaps they had followed the retreating ice until after tens of thousands of years they arrived in the country that we now call Germany (Figure 195). There is reason to believe that this man of Heidelberg could talk, but talk with difficulty.

Perhaps the men of the Ice Age came to Europe in several waves of migration during thousands of years, for we find that their ways of living changed rather suddenly from time to time, as if there had been new arrivals from Asia with new ideas. Historical America has been settled in about the same way, but during a much shorter period. You know that in some of our cities the first European settlers were English. The next wave of migration a hundred years later was Irish, and finally a third migration of Italians came, perhaps fifty years later. The English, Irish, and Italians, though all belonging to the

European race, have slightly different ways of living. So it may be that many of the successive waves of early man which overran Europe during the Pleistocene Period were all related to a primitive Asiatic race.

HEIDELBERG MAN

Figure 195. He probably closely resembles our ancestors of his time, for he was a member of the family. Therefore we should give this portrait a position in our ancestral halls. After a model by the Belgian artist Mascre under the direction of Prof. A. Rutot of Brussels. From *Men of the Old Stone Age* by H. F. Osborn.

Just as we speak of waves of English, Irish, or Italian immigrants, so these successive settlers in Europe have received separate names. Among the first and most primitive are the Chelleans, named after the place where their stone tools were first found. They lived in Europe during the warm period that followed the third series of glaciers that spread over the land. The flint tools or scrapers that the Chelleans have left behind them show that they used the fur of such animals as the reindeer and bear to keep themselves warm. All the flints they have left in their camps and caves were apparently used for domestic purposes. No arrowheads or spear points have been found. They probably used a pointed stick for a spear, but they knew nothing about the bow and arrow.

The invention of even crude clothing was one of the most important achievements of the primates. Apparently the progressive· primates who gradually became men had lived for so many million years in a warm climate that they had almost completely lost their own fur —we still have a little on the tops of our heads. If, then, they were to follow their favorite game into countries where there was snow and ice in winter, they must devise some form of clothing.

About this time primitive man made another invention of far-reaching importance. It was the use of fire. This invention also was probably made primarily for warmth. Later, of course, primitive men and women learned to prefer roasted meat to raw meat.

Both fire and clothing were probably used by primitive men and women long before the Chelleans appeared in Europe. It may be that even the Piltdown Man at the close of the Pliocene Period was acquainted with those two approaches to civilization. Perhaps these inventions were made in Asia and brought to Europe, Africa, Australia, and America by successive waves of migrating primates. We only know that the first undisputed evidences of well-formed flint tools for dressing skins and, according to Hugo Obermaier, the first clear evidences of the use of fire are found in the old Chellean camps and caves of Europe.

Then came the fourth great glacier, which covered a large part of Europe with ice for perhaps 100,000 years. This series of glaciers, radiating from the Alps and from Scandinavia, moved so slowly that for thousands of years the climate grew colder very gradually. It was during this time that a new group of tribes came into Europe and apparently displaced the old Chellean inhabitants. We call them Acheuleans. They have left behind them better flint tools than the Chelleans could make. They must have been better fighters, too, for all traces of the old Chelleans disappeared with the appearance of the Acheuleans.

The next invasion of Europe which we know about was made by men certainly more intelligent and perhaps more numerous. It was just before the fourth and last advance of the glaciers that these men, wonderful for those days, entered Europe. It may be that they came from Asia Minor, crossed the Bosphorus where Constantinople now stands, and entered Europe by walking up the broad valley of the Danube. Remains of these men have been found in a cave in Palestine by John Garstang of the University of Liverpool and in the Danube valley by

EVEN THE BEARS KNEW THIS WAS THE STONE AGE

Figure 196. The Heidelberg man couldn't buy ready-made fur coats. He had to kill the bear, eat the meat, and make his own coat. From *Weltall und Menschheit*, edited by Hans Kraemer.

other explorers. This immigration is called Mousterian, and the people of this race are called Neanderthals (Figures 196 and 197). There is some reason to believe, ac-

Courtesy of the American Museum of Natural History

NEANDERTHAL MAN

Figure 197. If we are not careful our dining-room will be too small to hold all our ancestral portraits, for here is another one—at least some of this gentleman's cousins married some of our ancestors. It is claimed that some people in Europe by the shape of their heads show their descent from the Neanderthal man. After a photograph of a head modeled by J. H. McGregor of the American Museum of Natural History.

cording to W. J. Sollas of Oxford University, that when these Neanderthals went northwest to Europe others of the same or similar race went southeast to Australia and Tasmania, where they lived until the white man came and caused their extinction. We call them Tasmanians and Australian savages.

Many places in Europe where they lived during the Mousterian epoch have been investigated, and the charred remains of their feasts have been found (Figure

Courtesy of J. M. Dent and Sons, Ltd.

CAVE-DWELLERS

Figure 198. From a drawing by E. P. Bucknall in *Nebula to Man* by H. R. Knipe, published by J. M. Dent and Sons, Ltd., London.

198). We know what animals they liked to eat, but do not think for a moment that the meat they ate was always fresh. Meat so old that we could not have it within smelling distance was probably enjoyed by them at their feasts. When these men of Europe had finished eating a carcass, they just threw what was left a short distance from their camp fire. They had no garbage heap which they burned or kept carefully covered with earth. The smell of badly decayed remains did not, apparently, disturb them. Around one of their camps the bones of a couple of thousand animals have been found, buried by the sands of ages, but lying as they had been thrown by these Neanderthal men of the Mousterian epoch. We must not be hard on these early Europeans, for the primitive savages of today are much like them, as any one knows who has seen and smelled an Eskimo in his tent. From evidence found in one cave it seems likely that on certain occasions these Neanderthal men ate each other.

The Neanderthal men and women came to Europe at an unfortunate time. The fourth and last great glacier was commencing to cover much of the land. Since these Neanderthals of the Mousterian immigration did not know how to build warm houses, they lived in caves, where they could keep large fires burning at the entrances. Mankind made little progress during the thousands of years of the fourth invasion of the Pleistocene ice. The weather was so blustering and food so hard to get that the Mousterians seem to have grown less intelligent during these trying times. They did not make their stone tools so well at the end of the icy period as they did at the beginning. There is also some evidence that so much confinement in dark, damp caves affected their health. Whatever the reasons may have been, the Neanderthal of the Mousterian migration was not able to resist the next great wave of mankind which entered Europe.

Apparently Europe was invaded this time from two directions and by two somewhat different types of mankind. A tall race, standing more erect than the Neanderthals, perhaps came from the east and entered Europe through the historic gateway, the Danube valley. The other race came from Africa, crossed the Mediterranean on those land bridges, and occupied southern Europe. These Africans were small, with negroid characteristics. Their large associates, too, may have had a few negro ancestors.

During the next epoch, called Aurignacian, these two races occupied Europe. The old Neanderthals disappeared. Most of them probably perished while fighting the new invaders, for the Aurignacian people used a wonderful invention, the bow and arrow; yet in some cases there is evidence that the Neanderthals lived in the same camp with the conquerors for a time (Figure 199).

These two races which dwelt in Europe during the Aurignacian epoch produced the first artists of whom we have any knowledge. Their drawings were made on the smooth rock walls in the caves. At first the pictures were crudely drawn, but the race grew more skilful as each thousand-year period was added to its history.

For thousands of years these two races, witnessing, it may be, the very dawn of art in the human race, occupied Europe. The more they decorated their caves and drew pictures on stag's horns and on ivory, the more skilful they became. So far as we know, only once was their possession of Europe seriously disputed. That disturbance was for a brief time when a tribe of good fight-

LIFE IN AN AURIGNACIAN CAMP

Figure 199. When the first tall men of the Aurignacian epoch entered Europe they lived in huts but made their drawings in caves. From *Every Day Life in the Old Stone Age* by Marjorie and C. H. B. Quennell, published by G. P. Putnam's Sons, New York.

ers came up the valley of the Danube as the Neanderthal man had done tens of thousands of years before. These new men are called Solutreans. They made poor pictures but very sharp spears. For a short while, apparently, they ruled Europe, and then they disappeared.

CRO-MAGNON MAN

Whether they were driven away or killed we do not know.

We do know that again artistic races occupied Europe. Those little men and women from northern Africa still

CRO-MAGNON MAN

Figure 200. After a photograph of a head modeled by J. H. McGregor of the American Museum of Natural History.

lived in southern Europe, for they never had been driven out by the Solutreans. In the north and central parts we find the remains of a tall giant race very much like their predecessors. We call them Cro-Magnons (Figure 200). They may have been cousins but not descendants of the original big men of the Aurignacian epoch. There is some evidence that these tall and erect Cro-Magnons first appeared in Spain and then spread west and northwest through Europe. With the Cro-Magnons in this epoch was a shorter race that bears some resemblance to our modern Eskimo.

The second epoch in the life of these artistic races is called the Magdalenian. In no other period in any part of the earth did early man produce such works of art. These Magdalenian artists of the Cro-Magnon race used colors in making lifelike pictures of animals (Figures 201 and 202). They carved in ivory (Figure 203) and modeled in clay (Figure 204).

Finally the Cro-Magnon men devised a way of representing a herd of reindeer without drawing each animal (Figure 205). Having started the picture of the herd with a few well-drawn deer, they found a series of lines sufficient to reproduce to the mind the idea of a stampeding herd of wild reindeer. They used the same impressionistic method to represent a herd of galloping horses.

While the Cro-Magnon men were developing this remarkable skill, and the women, perhaps, were using the bone needles (Figure 206) which have been found in their camps, the fourth and last great Pleistocene glacier was slowly withdrawing from Europe. For thousands of years this glacier, or to be more accurate this group of glaciers, slowly melted. In Switzerland some shrank

Courtesy of "The Illustrated London News"

CRO-MAGNON ARTISTS PAINTING THE BISON

Figure 201. By the light of oil lamps of which one or two have been found, these Cro-Magnon artists are painting on the walls of a cave. One man is grinding and mixing paint. This is an imaginary picture of life in the famous cave of Altamira, Spain. After a drawing by A. Forestier in *The Illustrated London News* of August 10, 1912.

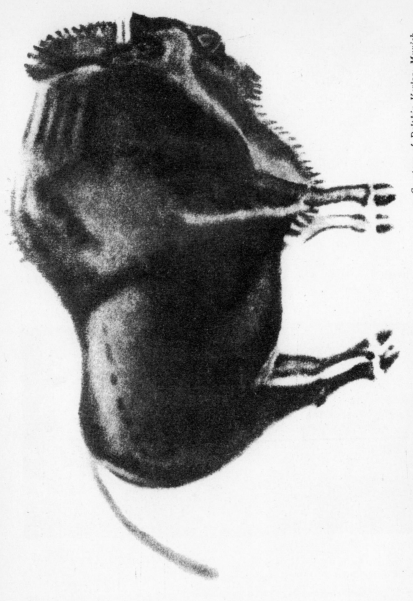

A BISON DRAWN BY A CRO-MAGNON ARTIST

Figure 202. Several colors were used by the artist when he made this drawing in the cave of Altamira, _____ ___ ___ l__t exhibits of Cro-Magnon art. From *Die Maleren der Eiszeit* by

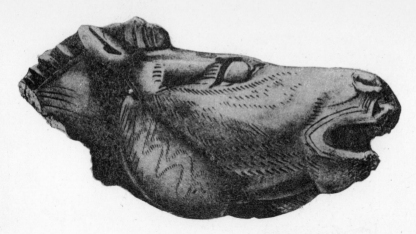

HEAD OF A HORSE BY A CRO-MAGNON ARTIST

Figure 203. The artist used a reindeer antler from which to carve this head. Found in Mas d'Azil on the bank of the Arize, France. From *Die Malerei der Eiszeit* by Herbert Kuhn.

BISON MODELED IN CLAY BY A CRO-MAGNON ARTIST

Figure 204. Some clay models have been found which were apparently used as targets for their spears. Perhaps the hunter always attacked a clay image just before he attacked the wild animal. It was probably a ceremony connected with some superstition. From *Die Malerei der Eiszeit* by Herbert Kuhn.

away up the valleys between the remnants of those majestic folds that had risen in the Miocene Period. The slowly moving ice-sheets that are so characteristic of Alpine scenery today are merely miniature images of their giant predecessors. In northern Germany and Great Brit-

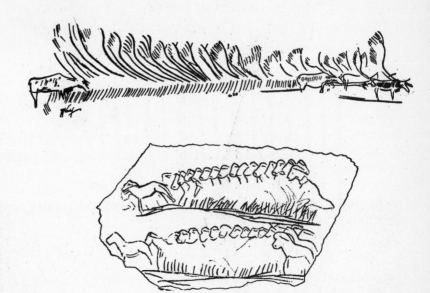

Courtesy of the American Museum of Natural History

IMPRESSIONISTIC DRAWINGS

Figure 205. Toward the close of their artistic career, the Cro-Magnon men devised this modern method of drawing herds of horses and reindeer.

ain the glaciers withdrew toward the north, and there beyond the Arctic Circle we find them today. This withdrawal of the last Pleistocene glaciers was not uniform. There were times when for a hundred years or more the glaciers grew neither larger nor smaller. We have a similar situation today, for we find the glaciers of Switzerland have changed very little in size during the period of modern history. Then there were times when the glaciers grew larger and extended farther down the valleys or, in Germany and Great Britain, covered more land. The glaciers, like huge frozen monsters, seemed reluctant to retreat from Europe and North America under the repeated

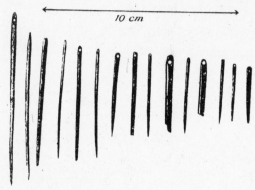

Courtesy of the American Museum of Natural History

BONE NEEDLES USED BY CRO-MAGNON WOMEN
Figure 206. Found in the grotto of Lacave in southern France.

attacks of the increasingly warm air. Just as the air had always won in its conflict with the mountains, so the warm atoms of O and N gradually melted the ice and drove the glacier to its final stand near the tops of the high mountains and in the distant polar regions.

With the withdrawal of the glaciers great changes in the weather probably took place throughout the world. During the Cro-Magnon epoch and presumably for a long time before that period the country we now call

Egypt enjoyed a moist climate with many storms and plenty of rain. The great Nile River, destined to be so famous, had dried up because the sources of the river in far-off Abyssinia and Central Africa were nearly dry. Strange rivers ran across the old Nile valley from the hills which lie to the east and along the edge of the Red Sea.

With the disappearance of the glaciers the weather changed. Abyssinia had once more a season of heavy rainfall. This rain water drained into the numerous rivers that make the sources of the Nile, which again flowed north through its historic valley to the Mediterranean Sea. The winds which brought rain to Egypt and caused those rivers to flow from the Red Sea hills across the Nile valley disappeared. A dry northerly wind took their place, and Egypt became again the sandy waste with which we are now so familiar.

The return of the Nile to its former glory took place about 12,000 B.C. The glacier left the northern shores of Germany about 15,000 B.C. and in its retreat north finally abandoned the southern shores of Sweden about 10,000 B.C. For reasons that we cannot give in this story these dates are known with fair accuracy. However, more important to us than these dates or the movements of the glacier are the great migrations of primitive men that were apparently caused by changing weather. Perhaps the interior of Asia grew dry so that the animals were forced to seek food to the west in Europe and to the east in North America. In that case the meat-eating primates would certainly follow the animals.

Whatever the cause, the artistic career of the Cro-Magnon people came to a close with the invasion into Europe of primitive men from Russia and Asia. They came up the valley of the Danube River, and they came along the shores of the Baltic Sea. They were better fighters than the Cro-Magnons and had sharper spears. These invading warriors were soon followed by men who had domestic dogs and knew how to make dishes out of clay (Figure 207).

Once before, the life of these cave artists had been interrupted by the Solutrean warriors. Finally, at the time of the appearance of the modern Nile and the disappearance of the old glacier, the Cro-Magnons were crushed by the invading hordes of fighters from Russia and Asia. Yet they were not exterminated as were their predecessors, the Neanderthal men. Although no longer making remarkable pictures and statues, they lived with their conquerors. Even today there is some reason to believe there are thousands of people in southern France who are descended from that wonderful race of artists.

Now we have almost reached the epoch when human beings kept records. Ten thousand years more or less bring us to the present time. During this interval man has made tremendous progress. Like the mammals and reptiles of old, he has migrated in large numbers from one continent to another. Since he can sail over the ocean,

MEN OF THE NEW STONE AGE

Figure 207. Here we have the hunters and warriors who conquered the Cro-Magnon men. Perhaps this picture represents a hunting scene on the shores of the Baltic Sea. They may be on their long journey from Russia to France and Spain about 10,000 years ago. From *Weltall und Menschheit*, edited by Hans Kraemer.

he no longer needs the ancient land bridges, some of which have sunk beneath the sea. The animals, however, have changed very little since Cro-Magnon man drew pictures of horses on the walls of his cave.

One of the principal reasons for this lack of change is the shortness of the time. We must always remember that it usually takes millions of years to bring about important changes in animals, as well as in mountains. Also in this very brief period of a few thousand years there have been no marked changes in climate. No great mountain chains have risen or disappeared. No large land mass has sunk beneath the sea or risen from it. No new glacier has spread over the land. Therefore, there is no reason why most of the animals should change in so short a time.

Why some men have grown so wonderfully clever in this historic period is a question we cannot discuss in this book. Perhaps some day you will read such books as *Character of Races* by Ellsworth Huntington and learn why some tribes of human beings are so bright and powerful.

We have covered 1,000 million years or more of the earth's history. We did not start at the beginning, and now we must bring our story to a close before we have reached the present time.

This...
to t...
l-a-...
chap...

XX. AN IMAGINARY PERIOD

We have finished our story. We started when the earth was a magnificent ball, huge shooting stars were falling into a boiling ocean, the clouds were brilliant with lightning, and thunder echoed among the newly made mountains as the earth squirmed and writhed under the blows from those falling stars. It was a wonderful time, when only the laws of physics and chemistry were in control.

Then as Sam and the rest of us traveled down through the museums of time, we saw germs appear in the warm fresh water of those very early oceans. If we had hovered over the earth for a longer time we might have seen some group of flashing shooting stars smash into the earth with such a blow as to kill all the little germs. We might have become tired waiting for the germs to come again, and perhaps we would have gone off to one of the other earths which are up in the sky and look like stars. Such a journey might have taken millions of years, and when we had returned to our own earth we might have found the oceans again warm, the sun shining once more through the clouds, and the germs again struggling in the shallow seas.

AN IMAGINARY PERIOD

Perhaps several times germs started to live in those ancient seas, and perhaps each time they were destroyed by brilliant, roaring, shooting stars which were falling on the earth. At last they were able to live and were disturbed no more.

We saw life become a cell, then a group of cells. In turn there have appeared before us the fish, the amphibian, the reptile, and the mammal. Finally from among the mammals there appeared the primates and from among the primates the European white primates who founded the British Empire and the United States of America.

We have watched mountain ranges come and go. Several times we have shivered as we realized that glaciers were creeping down over a large part of the earth. Through long ages we have seen great stretches of land slowly disappear beneath the ocean, and then we have welcomed other land masses as they rose from the sea.

Do you suppose we all realize how long these changes have taken—how very, very slowly the earth moves and the animals change? The whole history of America and even of Europe is but a day compared with the time that has passed since primates first came down from trees in search of food.

Perhaps you are still puzzled by that perplexing question we have encountered so frequently: Why do some animals develop new shapes and habits, while at the same time their cousins do not change at all? Apparently no animal ever changes his shape very much unless starvation or death continually selects certain ones that are different from their brothers and sisters; then, after ages, new animals are evolved. From time to time you will probably read a great deal about our family history. You will hear many reasons given why we are no longer little single cells as our early ancestors were.

As we have examined the earth in this imaginary journey, we have seen our ancestors change from using fins to using feet and walking on the dry ground. Then they stood on their hind legs and developed hands. During all this time they had some brains—very little, to be sure, and that little badly scattered in different parts of the body. As they grew more intelligent the brain became centered more and more in the head, until finally the brain grew more powerful than the muscles. We do not mean that the brain and muscles are at all alike. We mean that there are usually two ways of doing many things. First, an animal can accomplish his purpose by brute force, or, secondly, he can accomplish the same thing by using his brains. *Tyrannosaurus rex* and Smilodon used brute force principally, but the white primates use their brains and are therefore more powerful than the dinosaur or the saber-tooth tiger. Perhaps the most important period in the history of the earth since the first appearance of the little germs was when the primates developed so much brain that they could conquer their enemies and get their food better by the use of their intelligence than by the use of their muscles.

For nearly 1,000 million years life survived earthquakes and glaciers by means of a very small amount of brains, and as you look around among your fellow citizens you will find that many today flourish amid the accidents and turmoil of modern life with a surprisingly small amount of that latest feature of animal evolution.

It may have been 100 million years ago that ants and bees developed a wonderful intelligence. Five or 10 million years ago bears and beavers developed a considerable amount of brain and therefore showed intelligence in their conduct. Finally, primates began to develop brains and to use their intelligence. The primates had a great advantage over their brain-producing predecessors, for their life in trees developed the hands. They were able to hold clubs and stones and so could make and use tools.

Fortune favored the white primates, while the ants, the bees, the beavers, the elephants, and the grizzly bears had hard luck. Each in turn developed surprising ability, but for various reasons each failed to conquer the world as the white primate has done. In a very amusing little book, *This Simian World*, Clarence Day tries to imagine what this world would have been like if the cat family had won in the contest and had become the supreme animal on the earth. Then in turn he discusses the qualities good and bad of the other great families which might have conquered the earth, such as the elephant family. It is probably good for us to play with these imaginary scenes, for it makes us more appreciative of the excellent characteristics of some of the great animal families, as, for example, the cleanliness of the cat, the patience of the elephant, and the organizing ability of the ant. Also as we look about us we then begin to realize that we have certain family traits received from our own great animal family, the primates.

Since we are resting now from that long journey during which we jumped like geological goats from period to period, let us sit cozily on the side of a phantom volcano and imagine another situation.

When those shooting stars were falling and forming the earth, let us assume that they had formed at the same time 100 other earths all just like ours. Then let us suppose that germs had appeared in the warm and shallow water of each of these earths. Do you suppose that a white primate would have been developed on each of those 100 earths? If such a queer animal had appeared on each earth, would he have required 1,000 million years to develop in each case as he did on our earth? Of course we don't know, but now that we are resting we can talk it over. Let us each have our own opinion, but you can read mine, for I am writing it here in this book. Of course that does not mean that mine is better than yours.

My guess is that not on a single other earth would a white primate like us have appeared. On many of those

Let us assume...100 other earths

earths animals with brains would have been developed. Perhaps on a few earths the ruling and conquering family of animals would have been much more intelligent than we are. If they should meet us they might think us crude and savage. They would say that our cruelty to each other and our fondness for fighting are due to our ancestors' having lived in trees in a jungle only a few million years ago.

It was only recently that the primates on this earth became so developed that their brains were more powerful than their muscles. Ants and bees developed marvelous brains earlier by 100 million years than we, but while ants nearly succeeded, they nevertheless failed to conquer the world. In some of these other imaginary earths, the ruling family might have developed a brain more powerful than muscles much earlier in their history. Compared with the primates on this earth, that early development would give them an immense advantage, so that if we visited such an earth we would find the ruling family of animals much more civilized than we are.

Since we have become supreme on this earth only after some 1,000 million years of struggle, it is not only possible but even very probable that on many of those 100 imaginary earths, we would find no animal family supreme. Perhaps it would take another interminable age for most of those earths to evolve a family of animals that could really be rulers. In many cases such supremacy might never appear. In perhaps most cases one powerful family might follow another without ever developing an extraordinary amount of brains. We have seen the amphibian succeeded by the family of dinosaurs; then came the saber-tooth tigers and the mastodons. In a similar way other earths might have continued until they all became cold and frozen as the sun grew dark.

As time goes on, the leading primates of this earth will probably become both happier and more powerful. By "more powerful" we do not mean that they will build greater navies and taller buildings. We mean that they will know more about themselves and about each other. Then they will become more sensible. They won't quarrel so much with each other, and large groups of primates will seldom fight other large groups in organized war. The ants, the originators of organized warfare, will some day be the only fauna to maintain it. The primates will learn that by coöperation they can rule the earth more effectively than by fighting among themselves. This ruling of the earth is no easy matter for the white primates, for the bacteria which cause disease must be destroyed, and the insects must be prevented from killing our plants and trees.

With greater security and better health we will probably be happier and more friendly with each other. This being at peace with the other primates on the earth will probably be the most important achievement of all. Apparently such a condition will come only when we have greater knowledge about ourselves and about life in general. The wars and the suffering have been caused in nearly all cases by ignorance. The more intelligent we become, the more tolerant we shall be of other people and the more we shall object to the old inherited tendency to get what we want when we want it by killing a number of our enemies and seizing their property.

As the white primates continue to add to their vast store of knowledge, they may learn as much about life as they know about electricity. Then they may do amazing things; one primate may be able to communicate with another by thought transference; they may be able to concentrate that curious phenomenon we call life to such an extent that they will prolong each primate's life by a hundred years.

Of course all this happiness may not come to pass. Perhaps, for aught we know, the sun may grow a little cooler; that is, temporarily so for a few million years. Under such conditions even the Eskimo might perish, and the amphibians would once more be the rulers of the earth. The primates might die as the old dinosaurs did at the end of the Cretaceous Period.

Let us take a more cheerful and also a more probable view. Apparently we are approaching an interglacial period, when in some thousands of years Greenland will have as many forests and flowers as Tennessee now has. Also we are rapidly learning about ourselves and the origin of our customs and ideas. We are becoming less superstitious. Instead of being afraid of the people of

WEATHER REPORT
Colder to-night
and tomorrow, and for
the next million
years
K·M.

THE END OF OUR JOURNEY

another nation we are learning to like them. Such things tend to make us happier, and they all come from learning more about the earth and the curious animals, including the white primates, that live on its surface. If you wish to, you can try to find the answer to a few of those puzzling problems that we have found only half solved as we studied the events of the past.

Some day, when you read about astronomy, you will learn that there may be millions of earths among the stars. On tens of thousands of these earths there may be animal families whose brains have become more powerful than their muscles, and some of these families may be very much our superiors. You will also learn, perhaps, when you read about the stars, how the sun was formed and what will become of this earth and all its flora and fauna. That is a very interesting but a very different subject, so that now, Sam, we must leave that cozy volcano and bring to an end the long journey we have taken together down through the geological ages.

INDEX

INDEX